BODYART HOLIDAYS U.S.A.

by Carol Hauswald and Alice Maskowski
illustrated by Susan Pinkerton

In memory of Bobbie,
who taught us the pioneer spirit

Publisher: Roberta Suid
Editor: Carol Whiteley
Design & Production: Susan Pinkerton
Cover Art: David Hale

On-line address: MMBooks@AOL.com

Entire contents copyright © 1996 by Monday Morning Books, Inc.
For a complete catalog, please write to the address below.

P.O. Box 1680, Palo Alto, CA 94302

Monday Morning is a registered trademark of
Monday Morning Books, Inc.

Permission is hereby granted to reproduce
student materials in this book for non-commercial
individual or classroom use.

1-878279-95-5
Printed in the United States of America
987654321

CONTENTS

Introduction   4

What Is BodyArt?   6

Honoring Animals   7

Embracing the Earth   23

Honoring Explorers   33

Let's Hear It for Leaders!   45

A Tribute to Tribes   55

Happy Birthday, America!   69

INTRODUCTION

A proud eagle soaring free, his wings the outlines of a child's hands. An "Imagination Animals" bulletin board featuring the tracings of many tiny fingers. Paper moccasins that are outlines of a child's feet and can actually be worn.

The pages that follow provide models and simple directions that will enable you and your children to produce these and many other special-day creations based on hands, fingers, feet, toes, and other body parts. You'll also find related bulletin boards, crafts, songs, action verses, games, and snacks that turn *BodyArt* into a whole-learning environment that fosters imagination and self-esteem.

Celebrating Celebrations

The multi-sensory approach to learning that *BodyArt* incorporates focuses on six special-day units:

Honoring Animals. Are there really special days set aside to pay tribute to animals? The answer is a resounding yes! Animals in many countries are honored, and *BodyArt* includes the larger ones, lions and giraffes. Mid-sized animals are featured too—the deer and the dog—while the tiny turtle and frog complete the unit's "circle of life."

Embracing the Earth. This special occasion is a combination Earth Day/Arbor Day in which even young children learn that they too can help protect Mother Earth. This unit's activities are designed to reinforce a child's natural love for flowers, trees, and good things to eat.

Honoring Explorers. Children will enjoy moving through time and space as they make projects that give them a sense of history. Projects the children can look forward to include Columbus's *Santa Maria* sailing ship, the Wright brothers' plane *The Flyer*, and making footsteps on the moon like those of the Apollo 11 astronauts.

Let's Hear It for Leaders! Children learn in this unit that a leader is someone who guides or directs others and that leadership is not limited to a specific gender or ethnicity. *BodyArt* activities reflect the independence, dedication, and commitment needed to be a good leader—from making a "Follow the Leader" bulletin board to providing a helping hand to others.

A Tribute to Tribes. American Indian Day was first celebrated on May 13, 1916, at the request of Sherman Coolidge, an Arapahoe Indian. Since that time, much has been done to dispell the Indian stereotype, and this *BodyArt* unit continues that work. Activities introduce children to tribal diversity; projects such as making moccasins, rain sticks, and sand paintings engage children's interest and help show an appreciation for cultures.

Happy Birthday, America! Some call it Independence Day. Others simply call it the Fourth of July. Whatever you prefer, it's the time for a great birthday celebration. Learning about and participating in this holiday will complement your summer festivities curriculum, with such projects as *BodyArt* bells, Statue of Liberty crowns, and patriotic ice cream cones.

Literature Links

Each unit of *BodyArt: Holidays U.S.A.* includes a list of picture book read-alouds. These books will awaken and sustain children's interest in language and in the subject matter covered. The books are sensitively written, beautifully illustrated, and age-appropriate; they make wonderful springboards to the units. Many of the read-alouds also tie directly to specific *BodyArt* projects. For example, after listening to *Imogene's Antlers* by David Small, the children make a *BodyArt* "Deer Me" antler headband.

The picture books may also be used as follow-ups to *BodyArt* activities. The stories will inspire creative drama, puppetry, spontaneous games, child-drawn picture books, movement songs, child-dictated stories, and more—activities that all contribute to whole-language learning.

All of the read-alouds listed are readily available through libraries and bookstores. Inexpensive paperback editions can often be purchased through children's book clubs. Two clubs that we use frequently are:

The Trumpet Club
666 Fifth Avenue
New York, NY 10103

Scholastic Inc.
730 Broadway
New York, NY 10003

Another good source for books is:
Sundance Distributors and
    Publishers
P.O. Box 1326
Newton Road
Littleton, MA 01460

Materials for the *BodyArt* Projects
The projects in this book require common arts and crafts supplies: nontoxic tempera or finger paints, crayons, washable markers, nontoxic glue, scissors, hole punches, poster board, construction paper, paper fasteners, and rolls of colored bulletin board paper. *Note:* When using tempera paint, mix with a small amount of Staflo starch. This makes the paint adhere better to paper, and eliminates flaking; it also gives a nice sheen to the finish. You can make your own low-cost finger paint by using a 50-50 mixture of tempera paint and starch.

Whenever possible, we recommend the use of recycled materials—items such as paper towel rolls, egg cartons, plastic milk bottles, cardboard from cereal boxes, and wallpaper samples. Using recycled supplies will keep student projects inexpensive—and make them earth-friendly too.

Where Do You Go from *BodyArt: Holidays U.S.A.*?
If you and your children enjoy the projects in this *BodyArt* book, you may also be interested in the five other books in the series: *BodyArt: Seasonal Holidays* covers Sukkot, Passover, Easter, April Fool's Day, Kwanzaa, New Year's Day, and Children's Day. *BodyArt: World Holidays* features holidays around the world. *BodyArt: People* deals with families, feelings, friends, and community. *BodyArt: Nature* features four-legged animals, birds, fish, insects, spiders, and seasons. And *BodyArt: Holidays* celebrates birthdays, Halloween and harvest time, Hanukkah and Christmas, and "I Love You Days." Together they form a solid curriculum with which you can involve your children in enjoyable learning all year long.

What Is BodyArt?

Like all activities that build self-esteem, *BodyArt* begins with the children. *BodyArt* projects are arts and crafts activities based on the young creator's hands, fingers, feet, toes, and other body parts. The outlines and shapes of these body parts are then enhanced with a wide variety of free or inexpensive crafts materials and transformed into special works of art.

But *BodyArt* projects are much more than simply coloring within the lines or filling in worksheets. Intricately woven into them are children's own imaginations and personal perceptions. When viewing a circle, adults see the shape; but a child who has just drawn a circle may see a hot air balloon, an iridescent bubble, or a turtle with its head and feet pulled in. *BodyArt* draws on young children's creativity, and allows children to make unique contributions to their own projects—because without their special bodies and minds, there would be no artwork. Final products, therefore, will be treasured for years as testaments to the children's talents and uniqueness.

The projects themselves are fun and easy to do. Colors are bright and brash, lines are big and bold, shapes are repeated over and over again. As the children work through the activities, they become involved in a magical world, one that's bursting with excitement and meaningful involvement and learning.

One of these types of learning is preparatory learning. The child learns how to cut with scissors, which is a prewriting skill. He or she also learns how to make marks on paper, which fosters eye-hand coordination.

Academic learning also takes place with *BodyArt* units. After a unit is completed, for example, children have a better notion about measurements and directions. Finally, each *BodyArt* unit is designed to be sensitive to the needs of gender, culture, and ecological considerations. And all *BodyArt* learning is child-friendly.

Activities are slanted toward children from preschool to grade 1. At the earliest developmental level, children will simply provide the necessary body part for tracing and cutting by the adult; they'll complete the project by decorating the shape. More advanced children can trace the shapes themselves and assist in the cutting, as well as decorate. Older children will be able to handle all the tasks on their own. But no matter how much of a project young artists do, their efforts will lead to increased confidence. Each "I did it" experience will motivate children to achieve at ever-higher levels of learning.

In a nutshell, *BodyArt*:

• uses language for real, meaningful purposes so that children are able to make sense of their world and their place in it;

• actively involves children through experiential, inductive, and democratic processes;

• recognizes the learning environment as a social community in which educational resources are found;

• incorporates a wide variety of tactile, kinesthetic, visual, and listening activities that reach all learning styles;

• is highly adaptable to the typical learner, as well as to gifted and talented and learning-challenged children.

HONORING ANIMALS

Many countries throughout the world pay tribute to animals. In Mexico, the Day of St. Anthony, which falls on January 17, is a special holiday to honor pets. Pets are given baths, dressed up in colorful ribbons, flowers, and bows, and then taken to church.

In the United States, the first Sunday in May is the beginning of Be Kind to Animals Week. This special occasion is devoted to caring for all creatures—great and small.

On May 22, the International Jumping Frog Jubilee is held. This uniquely American festivity was introduced in 1865 by the famous American writer and humorist Samuel Clemens—otherwise known as Mark Twain.

Start your animal celebration with a bulletin board of imaginary animals. Then move on to *BodyArt* lions, giraffes, deer, dogs, and turtles, which are featured in this unit. By unit's end, each child should be in possession of a "movable zoo" ready to be taken home and played with.

Imagination Animals Bulletin Board

Wuzzies live on land. Komokos live in caves. Jimmy Kongas swim in the sea, and Gee Lalas fly in the sky! Never heard of such creatures? Don't worry. They're imaginary! Your children will enjoy making up and creating critters while they play with language and increase their appreciation of words and meanings.

Materials: Markers or crayons, white poster board

Directions: Trace the childrens' hands on poster board in a variety of positions. Overlap the tracings. When the entire poster board is filled, ask the children to study the poster and use their imaginations. Do they see any strange animals hidden in the picture? (An adult may get imaginations rolling by pointing out two or three examples.) When several creatures have been identified, have the children draw faces on them. Color in solid backgrounds behind the animals so that they will be noticeable. Then let the children give the creatures names and special talents (running sideways, hopping on one foot) as well as a faraway place to live!

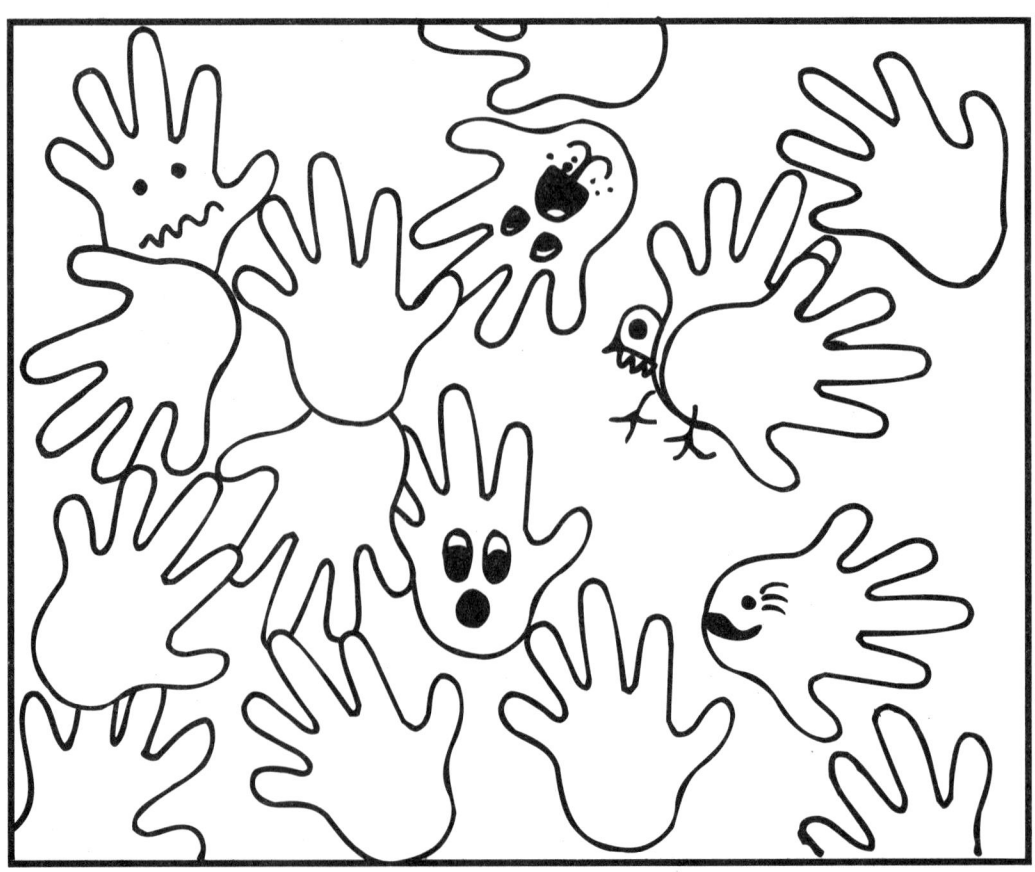

Soulful Sam

Use Eric Hill's *Where's Spot?* to introduce this project, and watch interest soar!

Materials: White construction paper, black construction paper, wiggly eyes, glue, scissors, ruler or wooden craft stick, black marker, pencil, masking tape

Directions: Trace the child's foot on a sheet of white construction paper. Cut out the entire foot, then trim the toe area so it has a smooth arch to it. Make a gumdrop-shaped nose in the center of the arch with black marker. Then glue wiggly eyes to the center of the paper foot. Cut out long balloon-shaped ears from black construction paper and glue to the sides of Sam's head. Tape a wooden craft stick or ruler to the back of Sam and have a puppet show!

The Jungle King

Big cats have always fascinated cultures, and this lion will entrance your children!

Materials: Large paper plate, brown construction paper, scissors, nontoxic glue, tan crayon, brown marker, pencil, ruler or wooden craft stick (optional), masking tape (optional)

Directions: To make the lion's mane, trace the child's hand (fingers apart) on a sheet of brown construction paper. Repeat five more times. Cut out the paper hands and glue around the perimeter of the paper plate, fingers extending outward. Bend the fingers forward for a three-dimensional look. Then add facial features with a marker, and tan fur with a crayon. If you want, tape a wooden craft stick or ruler to the back of the lion for a hand-held mask. Cut out eye holes big enough for children to see through.

Deer Me!

A good way to launch this activity is to read *Imogene's Antlers* by David Small. In the book, Imogene wakes up one morning with antlers growing out of her head. The story is so compelling that children will want to have antlers of their own!

Materials: Large paper plate; brown nontoxic, washable tempera; brush; brown or yellow construction paper; stapler and staples; scissors; transparent tape; pencil

Directions: Cut a hole in a paper plate large enough to sit comfortably on the child's head. Paint the plate with brown tempera. While the paint is drying, trace the child's hands on a sheet of brown or yellow construction paper. Cut out the paper hands. Fold the heel of one paper hand under 1/2" and position on the paper plate rim so it will sit above the child's ear. Staple the paper hand to the rim and put tape over any sharp edges. Repeat the process with the second "antler," positioning it so it sits above the child's other ear.

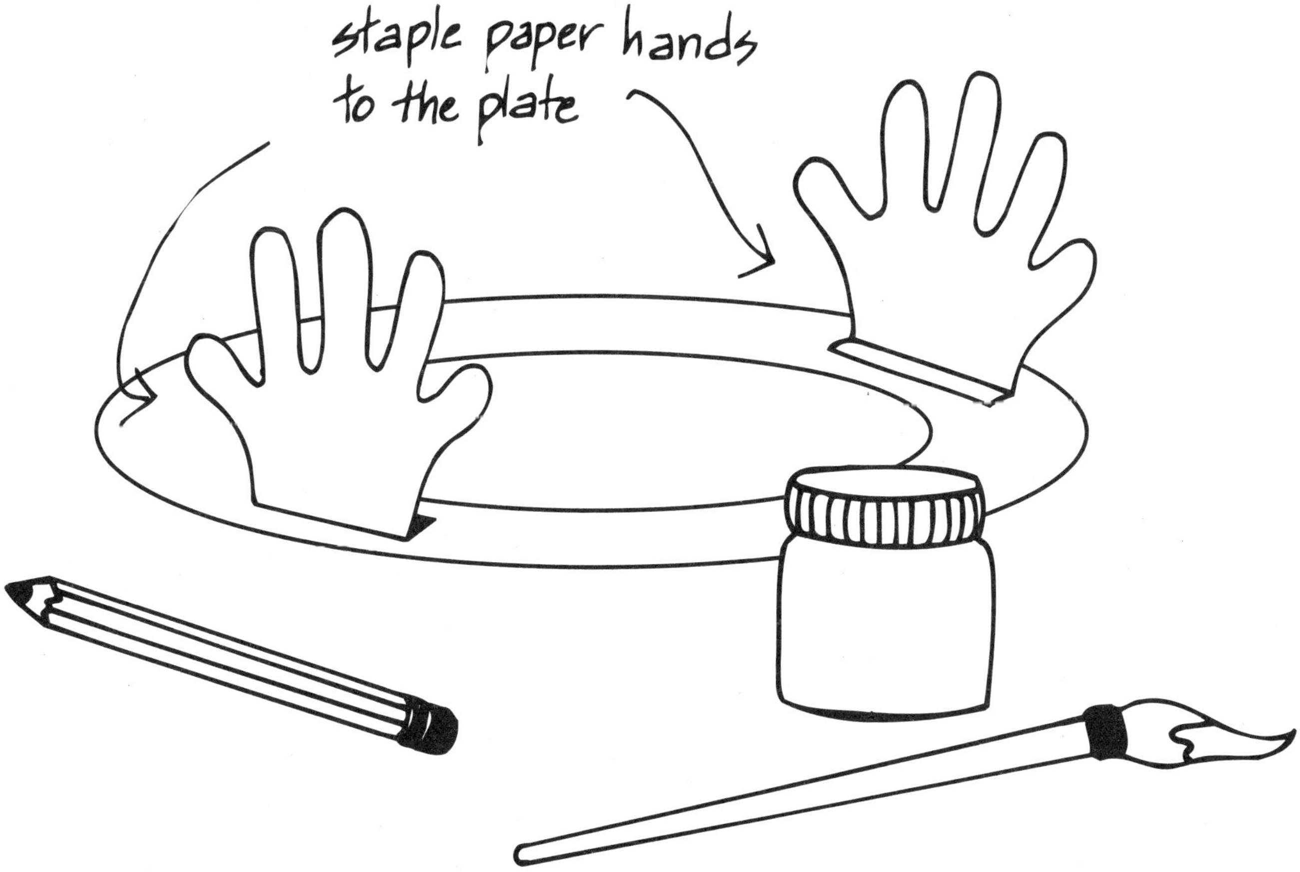

staple paper hands to the plate

Galloping Giraffe

You can start this project by reading Steve Zukmann's *It's a Good Thing...*, a hilarious account of how animals' shapes suit them.

Materials: 12" x 18" yellow construction paper, scissors, 4 paper fasteners, black marker, orange crayon, wiggly eyes, pencil, nontoxic glue, transparent tape, hole punch

Directions: Have the child hold his or her hand and arm in front of a sheet of yellow construction paper pinned vertically to the wall. The thumb should be tucked up, the four fingers closed and coming to a point, and the pinky extended slightly upward (see the illustration). Trace the child's hand and arm in this position and cut out. This is the giraffe's neck and head. To make the giraffe's body, cut out a yellow construction-paper oval and glue to the base of the giraffe's neck.

Cut out four 1"- wide by 2"- long rectangles of yellow construction paper for the giraffe's legs. Cut out a longer yellow rectangle for the giraffe's tail. Punch a hole through the top of each leg and through four spots along the bottom edge of the body. Insert a paper fastener through each leg and attach to the body so the legs will move. Fasten at the back and tape any sharp edges. Glue the tail to the end of the body. Orange squares can be drawn that let the yellow "skin" show through. Glue on wiggly eyes.

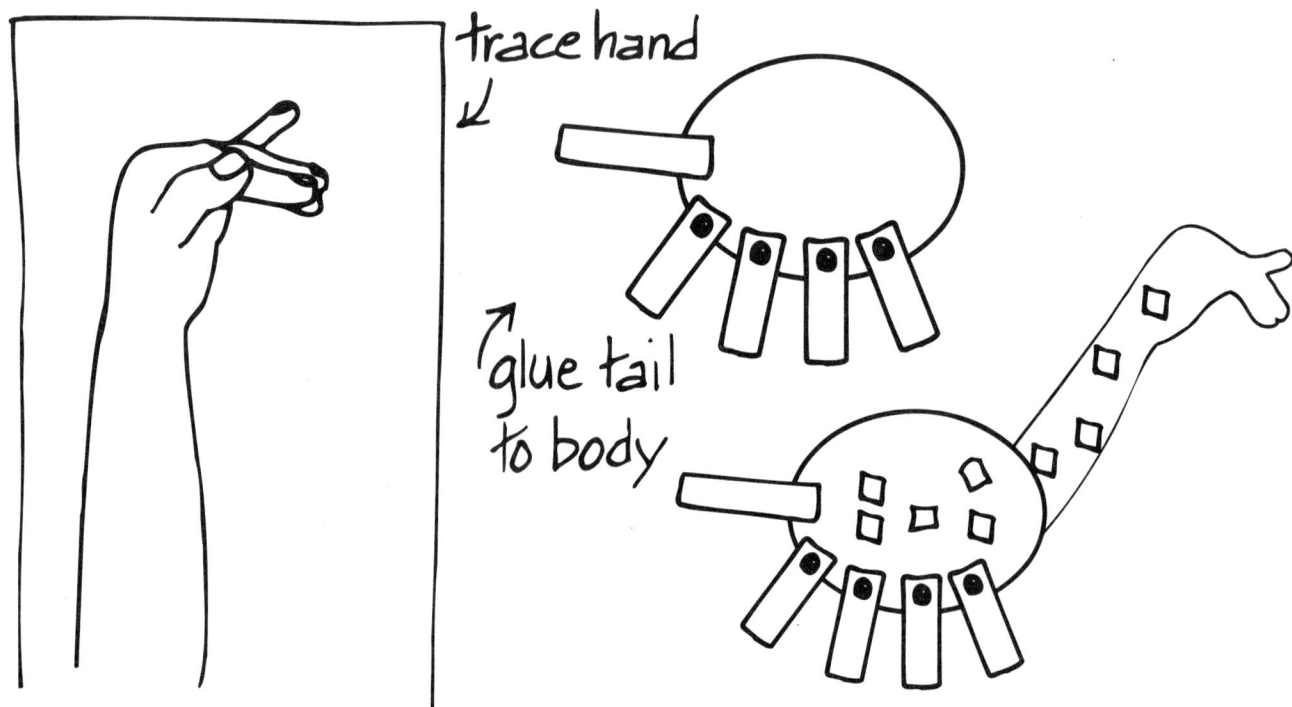

Lily Pad and Turtle

Start with the fantastic book *Jump, Frog, Jump!* by Robert Kalan. Add a *BodyArt* lily pad and turtle. Then you can have a wonderful water life jubilee!

Materials: Green construction paper, pink construction paper, 12" x 18" blue construction paper, pencil, scissors, wiggly eyes, empty brown plastic cupcake holder (from packaged cupcakes), glue

Directions: To make the lily pad, trace the child's hand (fingers together) on a sheet of green construction paper. Cut out the paper hand. Glue the "lily pad" to the center of the sheet of blue construction paper. Then cut out a small pink construction-paper flower head and glue to the lily pad's center.

To make the turtle, trace the child's hand (fingers apart) on a sheet of green construction paper. Cut out. Add wiggly eyes to the middle finger. Glue an empty cupcake container (bumpy side up) to the palm area. Then let the turtle swim for the lily pad!

Honoring Animals Finger Plays and Movement Songs

The Mushroom Song
(to the tune of "The Bear Went Over the Mountain")

(This is a movement song in which the animals get bigger and bigger. Read Mirra Ginsburg's *Mushroom in the Rain* [see the Read-Aloud section for details] to give children an even better idea of what this song is all about.)

The ant went under the mushroom,
The ant went under the mushroom,
The ant went under the mushroom
So the rain wouldn't get her all wet!

The butterfly went under the mushroom,
The butterfly went under the mushroom,
The butterfly went under the mushroom
So the rain wouldn't get her all wet!

The mouse went under the mushroom,
The mouse went under the mushroom,
The mouse went under the mushroom
So the rain wouldn't get him all wet!

The sparrow went under the mushroom,
The sparrow went under the mushroom,
The sparrow went under the mushroom
So the rain wouldn't get him all wet!

The rabbit went under the mushroom,
The rabbit went under the mushroom,
The rabbit went under the mushroom
So the rain wouldn't get him all wet!

The fox ran to the mushroom!
The fox ran to the mushroom!
The fox ran to the mushroom!
He wanted to find Rabbit there.

"No, we haven't seen him.
"No, we haven't seen him.
"No, we haven't seen him,
"And we've been here all day!"

So Fox ran from the mushroom,
Fox ran from the mushroom,
Fox ran from the mushroom
To see where Rabbit might be.

Rabbit thanked his new friends,
Rabbit thanked his new friends,
Rabbit thanked his new friends
For saving him from the fox!

Wake Up Lion Finger Play
(to the tune of "Are You Sleeping?")

Lion is sleeping, lion is sleeping.
Wake him up! Wake him up!
No, says the elephant!
No, says the hippo!
He'll eat us up! He'll eat us up!

Lion is sleeping, lion is sleeping.
Wake him up! Wake him up!
No, says the tiger!
No, says the leopard!
He'll eat us up! He'll eat us up!

Lion is sleeping, lion is sleeping.
Wake him up! Wake him up!
No, says the antelope!
No, says the mountain goat!
He'll eat us up! He'll eat us up!

Lion is sleeping, lion is sleeping.
Wake him up! Wake him up!
Yes, says the field mouse!
Yes, says the field mouse!
He's afraid of me! He's afraid of me!

This is the way we play with cat,
Play with cat, play with cat.
This is the way we play with cat
On Honoring Animals Day!

This is the way we dress up frog,
Dress up frog, dress up frog.
This is the way we dress up frog
On Honoring Animals Day!

This is the way we take care of them,
Take care of them, take care of them.
This is the way we take care of them
On Honoring Animals Day!

Animal Cheer

Two, four, six, eight,
Who do we appreciate?
Animals, animals, animals today!

Honoring Animals Song

(to the tune of "This Is the Way We Wash Our Clothes")

This is the way we brush our dog,
Brush our dog, brush our dog.
This is the way we brush our dog
On Honoring Animals Day!

This is the way we feed our fish,
Feed our fish, feed our fish.
This is the way we feed our fish
On Honoring Animals Day!

Honoring Animals Read-Alouds

Fiction

Asch, Frank. *Moongame.* New York: Scholastic, 1984.

Little Bird shows Bear a new game called Hide and Seek. Charmingly illustrated and available as a Big Book.

Bornstein, Ruth. *Little Gorilla.* New York: Ticknor & Fields, 1976.

The illustrations are delightful, the language is simple, the message is lovely—offspring are loved when they are babies, but they are loved when they grow up too!

Brett, Jan. *Annie and the Wild Animals.* Boston: Houghton Mifflin, 1985.

Annie's cat Taffy runs away so Annie looks for a new pet. But bigger and bigger wild animals want to become Annie's pet because she feeds them delicious corn cakes. Thankfully Taffy returns, bringing with her three soft, cuddly kittens!

Brett, Jan. *The First Dog.* San Diego: Harcourt Brace, 1988.

Jan Brett beautifully captures the landscape of the Ice Age with her illustrator's imagination. Kip is a cave boy and the Paleowolf is the ancestor of the modern dog. The story contains a nice mix of fiction and facts.

Brown, Marc. *Arthur's Tooth.* Boston: Little, Brown, 1985.

Even though Arthur is a mouse and not a child, youngsters will instantly relate to the rites of passage that accompany the loss of a first tooth. Look for the rest of the books in the Arthur series.

Brown, Ruth. *If At First You Do Not See.* New York: Holt, 1982.

Mama butterfly tells her caterpillar baby to eat leaves, but he goes to search for more appetizing meals! The picture book is read by turning it 360 degrees around!

Day, Alexandra. *Good Dog, Carl.* New York: Scholastic, 1985.

Mom puts Carl the dog in charge of the baby while she's gone. Carl is a great baby-sitter, and it's hilarious how human he is! Available as a Big Book.

Ehlert, Lois. *Color Zoo.* New York: Lippincott, 1989.

This Caldecott Honor recipient helps children learn shapes and names of animals. Big, bold, and child-friendly.

Gackenbach, Dick. *Harry and the Terrible Whatzit.* New York: Clarion Books, 1977.

The Whatzit is a terrible something that gets smaller and smaller once a young boy learns how to master his fear of it.

Galdone, Paul. *The Little Red Hen.* New York: Clarion Books, 1973.

The classic tale of the industrious hen who does all the work is still a favorite of young children. When the delicious cake comes out of the oven, Hen's roommates finally offer to help...eat it!

Gilman, Phoebe. *The Wonderful Pigs of Jillian Jiggs.* New York: Scholastic, 1988.

Jillian Jiggs never likes to clean up after herself. Her mom says her room looks like pigs live in it. This gives Jillian a great money-making idea—she makes pigs for the entire neighborhood! But can she give away her homemade creations? Instructions on how to make a pig are included.

Ginsburg, Mirra. *Mushroom in the Rain.* New York: Aladdin Books, 1974.

This oldie but goodie is a charming story that teaches interdependence in simple, easy-to-understand language. Children will love the humor as larger and larger animals seek cover under a mushroom.

Hill, Eric. *Where's Spot?* London: Ventura, 1980.

Young children love the Spot books, which come in all sizes and shapes. This edition is a tiny one that fits wonderfully well in small hands. Children get an opportunity to open doors, peek under beds, and look into chests as Mama looks for her baby puppy.

Hurd, Edith Thacher. *The Day the Sun Danced.* New York: Harper & Row, 1965.

Animals in winter are described in this offering that reads like poetry.

Jeschke, Susan. *Perfect the Pig.* New York: Holt, 1981.

A little pig wishes for wings and Olive, a girl artist, helps her friend fit in after he becomes a flying pig.

Kalan, Robert. *Jump, Frog, Jump!* New York: Scholastic, 1981.

Will Frog be able to jump away from his enemies? The suspense is wonderful, and so are the illustrations by Byron Barton. Available as a softcover Big Book.

Keats, Ezra Jack. *Hi, Cat!* New York: Aladdin Books, 1970.

Peter's new friend Cat is spoiling his neighborhood shows! But Peter comes to know that this is Cat's way of showing that he likes his human friend.

Kellogg, Steven. *Can I Keep Him?* New York: Dial, 1971.

A little boy keeps finding larger and larger animals to bring home—much to his mother's chagrin.

Korman, Justine (adapted by). *The Lion King.* New York: A Golden Book, 1994.

Disney's masterful story of how Simba the lion cub learns to assume his rightful place in the "circle of life" is told in this excellent offering.

Lobel, Arnold. *Fables.* New York: Harper & Row, 1980.

One-page short stories involve some 20 animals—from a crocodile in the bedroom to a mouse at the seashore. A Caldecott Medal winner.

Loomans, Diane. *The Lovables in the Kingdom of Self Esteem.* Tiburon, Calif.: H.J. Kramer, 1991.

In this charming picture book, animals like Mona Monkey, Bobbi and Billy Bear, and Elena Elephant teach children how to develop a "feel good" attitude about themselves.

Martin, Bill Jr. *Brown Bear, Brown Bear.* New York: Holt, 1983.

Wonderfully bright and bold illustrations by Eric Carle help tell this modern classic.

Prelutsky, Jack. *Zoo Doings.* New York: The Trumpet Club, 1983.

Animal poems that will tickle young childrens' funny bones. Illustrated by Paul O. Zelinsky.

Rylant, Cynthia. *Henry and Mudge.* New York: Bradbury Press, 1987.

This first book in the Henry and Mudge series tells how Mudge the dog brings happiness to a lonely child named Henry.

Sendak, Maurice. *Where the Wild Things Are.* New York: Harper & Row, 1963.

This classic tells the story of Max, a little boy who gets into so much mischief that his mom sends him to his bedroom. But Max winds up leading the Wild Things on a fantastic adventure.

Small, David. *Imogene's Antlers.* New York: Crown, 1985.

Imogene is a little girl who spends the entire day getting used to her new antlers! Just when her family thinks the problem is solved, though, another challenge arises.

Stadler, John. *Animal Cafe.* New York: Aladdin Books, 1980.

Maxwell thinks cash is magically showing up in his cash register. What's really happening is that his "lazy" cat and dog are cooking up an elaborate cafe every night after their owner goes home. A "Reading Rainbow" featured offering.

Stadler, John. *Hector the Accordion-Nosed Dog.* New York: Bradbury Press, 1983.

Hector's talented nose makes him a star—until he runs smack into a wall and his nose becomes an accordian!

Tresselt, Alvin. *The Mitten.* New York: Mulberry Books, 1964.

This old Ukrainian folk tale tells how a lost mitten in the forest becomes the home for larger and larger animals—until the mitten seam bursts!

Wildsmith, Brian. *Cat on the Mat.* Oxford: Oxford University Press, 1982.

Cat is good about sharing her mat until bigger and bigger animals start to come on board! The illustrations are wonderful!

Wildsmith, Brian. *Hunter and His Dog.* Oxford: Oxford University Press, 1989.

A hunter's dog teaches his owner to care for animals instead of shoot them.

Wildsmith, Brian. *The Lazy Bear.* Oxford: Oxford University Press, 1989.

A story about a kindly bear whose personality changes when he finds a wagon. He likes the ride down the hill, but bullies his friends to push the wagon up the hill.

Willard, Nancy. *Pish, Posh, Said Hieronymus Bosch.* New York: Trumpet Club, 1991.

Bosch was a real-life Dutch artist who loved odd creatures—much to the dismay, in this story, of the lady who looked after him and cleaned his house. The wonderful illustrations are by Leo and Diane Dillon.

Young, Ruth. *Golden Bear.* New York: Puffin Books, 1992.

Beautifully illustrated by Rachel Isadora, this excellent picture book tells of the special relationship between a young African-American child and his friend, a bear.

Zukmann, Steve and Henry Edelman. *It's a Good Thing...* Los Angeles: Price/Stern/Sloan, 1987.

Animals look the way they do for a good reason! This humorous offering illustrates the problems that would occur if storks got confused or if frogs didn't know how to jump. You may want to use this book as an introduction to the "Imagination Animals" bulletin board (p. 8). If you're unable to locate it, write to the publisher at 410 North La Cienega Boulevard, Los Angeles, CA 90048.

Nonfiction

Carwardine, Mark. *The Illustrated World of Wild Animals.* New York: Simon and Schuster, 1988.

Pictures of animals and their environments the world over are included in this comprehensive nonfiction offering.

Cole, Joanna. *A Chick Hatches.* New York: William Morrow, 1976.

Vivid photos show how a chick is hatched.

Cornell, Joseph. *Sharing Nature with Children.* Nevada City, Calif.: Dawn Publications, 1979.

Lots of different learning activities will help children appreciate nature while having a lot of fun. If the paperback is hard to locate, contact the publisher at 14618 Tyler Foote Road, Nevada City, CA 95959.

Forsyth, Adrian. *The Architecture of Animals.* Ontario: Camden House, 1989.

A fascinating look at how all sorts of small animals—from mice to beavers to fish, reptiles, and insects—make their homes and protect their young. The dramatic pictures will interest the children. If the book is hard to locate, contact the publisher at 7 Queen Victoria Road, Camden East, Ontario, Canada K0K 1J0.

Miller, Dorcas. *Track Finder.* Rochester, New York: Nature Study Guild, 1982.

A concise paperback guide to mammal tracks of the eastern and midwestern United States as well as eastern Canada. Clear, detailed drawings. If you have a hard time finding this book, contact the publisher at Box 10489, Rochester, NY 14610.

Pope, Joyce. *Do Animals Dream?* New York: Viking Kestrel, 1986.

Do animals feed their young? Why does the kangaroo have a pouch? Do all animals play? These and other questions are answered in this child-friendly resource.

Worthy, Judith. *Eyes.* Littleton, Mass.: Sundance Publishers & Distributors, 1988.

The big pictures and words are ideal to help young children learn how eyes reveal an animal's wants, needs, and character.

Honoring Animals Snacktime

Parade Edibles

Individual boxes of animal cookies are the special snack for this unit. But before eating the cookies, have children line up several animals and pretend there's a circus or parade coming to town. Then ask the children to imagine that an elephant, tiger, zebra, or other animal can talk. Ask, "What would the animal say?" "How would the animal's voice sound?" "How is the animal feeling today?" After the children have played for a bit, let them enjoy their cookies with a glass of milk.

Honoring Animals Game

Flipping Froggies

Flipping Froggies may become the children's new favorite game!

Materials: Flipping Froggies reproducibles (p. 22), lily pad (p. 13), crayons or markers, scissors, wiggly eyes, green construction paper (optional), glue

Directions: Copy, color, and cut out the reproducibles; glue each frog to green construction paper if sturdier frogs are needed. Fold each frog along the dotted lines (under by the mouth and head and up by the body, accordian style). You'll know the frogs are folded correctly if you press the back of the head and they jump! Glue on wiggly eyes for a very silly look.

When all the froggies are ready, it's time to play the Flipping Froggies game. Place the lily pad a short distance in front of four children. Line up all the froggies at the starting line. Then let each child gently press the head of one of the frogs and watch it jump. The first frog to land on the lily pad is the winner! Continue until every child has had a chance to race.

For extra fun, include the *BodyArt* turtles (p. 13) in the contest. Make them move by hiding a tiny wind-up toy under the cupcake container (to insert the toy, cut a hole in the container). Then have a race between the flipping froggies and the slow-motion turtles. Who will get to the lily pad first!

Note: For a large-motor game, put a blanket in the center of the room or yard and let the children "leap to the lily pad."

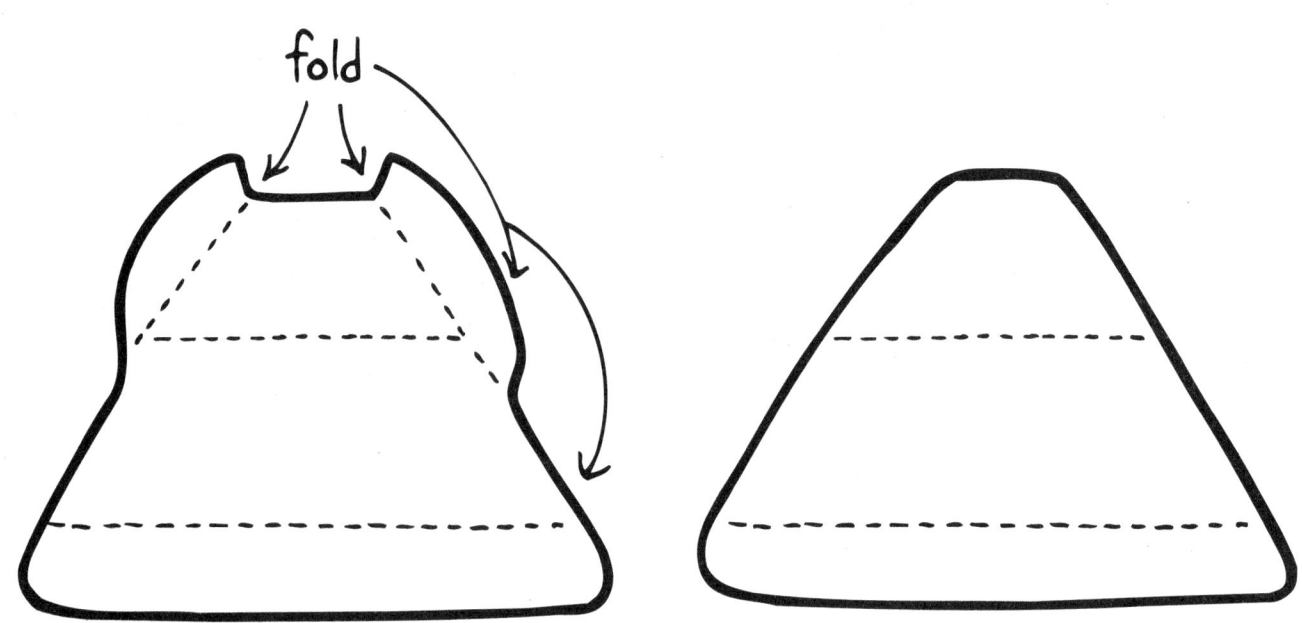

fold

glue on eyes

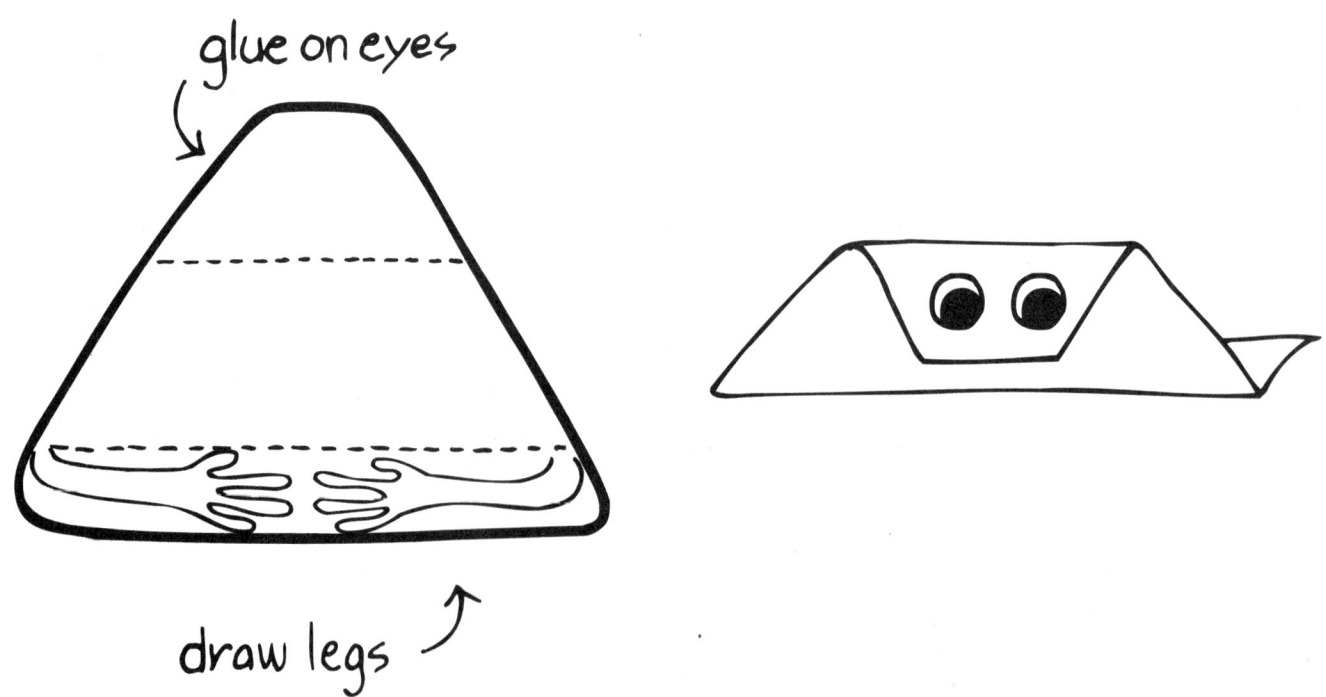

draw legs

EMBRACING THE EARTH

Most holidays are celebrated on only one day of the year. When it comes to celebrating the Earth, however, there are at least four special times. That's good news for those who have a strong commitment to teaching children about preserving natural resources.

The oldest holiday is America's Arbor Day. It was pioneered by J. Sterling Morton, who set out in the mid-1800s to plant trees in Nebraska. The original Arbor Day, for paying tribute to trees, was April 10, 1872. Three years later the holiday was moved to April 22, in honor of Morton's birthday.

Nearly 100 years later, on April 22, 1970, the first Earth Day was celebrated. On every April 22 since then, trees and all of Earth's natural resources are held in high honor. It's a time to celebrate everyone's commitment to preserving and protecting the environment.

On June 5 each year, World Environment Day is celebrated. On that day, water, forests, animals, and plants are especially spotlighted. The global event was first held in 1972 with representatives from 114 countries around the world.

Finally, there's Johnny Appleseed's birthday, on September 26. A frontier wanderer in the early 1800s, John Chapman became known to settlers of Pennsylvania, Indiana, and Ohio as the man who planted apple seeds.

Whatever day you choose to celebrate, *BodyArt* activities are a good springboard for introducing children to the new 3 R's of education—renew, reuse, recycle!

We Care for Mother Earth Bulletin Board

This bulletin board teaches even young children that they can make a difference simply by putting candy wrappers in the proper place.

Materials: World reproducible (p. 32); poster board; glue; scissors; nontoxic, washable tempera (blue, green, skin-tone colors); green and blue crayons; paintbrushes; paper fastener; marker; paint trays; transparent tape; small toys and "litter-type" items (candy wrappers, empty juice containers, etc.)

Directions: Enlarge the world reproducible. Glue to the poster board. Cut out the reproducible and color it with green and blue nontoxic tempera or crayons. Poke a hole through the center of the world and insert a paper fastener through it and the poster board. Secure the fastener at the back of the poster board. The world should be able to spin around.

To the right of the world, draw an empty trash can. Add the words "Our hands help keep Mother Earth clean." To the left of the world, draw an empty toy chest. Add the words "Our hands pick up toys."

Put a variety of skin-tone colors into the paint trays. Ask each child to dip his or her hand (palm down) into some paint and make prints on the world and above the trash can and toy chest. For the final touch, glue or tape tiny toys on the toy chest drawing and paper litter above the waste can.

Bountiful Apple Tree

Introduce this project by reading an appropriate book or talking about Johnny Appleseed (John Chapman). After the children finish making their trees, give them real red apples to eat. If you tell them you picked the apples from the trees they made, you'll be treated to a roomful of giggles!

Materials: Pieces of sponge approximately 2" wide by 1" deep; scissors; brown and green nontoxic, washable tempera; small red pompons; nontoxic glue; 12" x 18" white poster board; paint trays

Directions: Dip a sponge piece into a tray of brown paint. Make imprints up and down the sheet of white poster board (vertical position). At the base of this trunk area, make the imprints a bit longer and aiming downward for roots. Extend imprints outward from the mid-trunk area on both sides for branches. Let dry. To add leaves, ask the child to dip a hand (palm down) into a tray of green paint and make imprints (fingers apart) all around and across the treetop and branches. When all the paint is dry, glue red pompons throughout the leaf and branch areas. *Note:* If pompons are glued on white as well as green areas, the "apples" will stand out.

Whole World in Our Hands

Two hands can make a difference, and here's a project that proves it!

Materials: World reproducible (p. 32), scissors, green and blue markers or crayons, construction paper in skin-tone colors, 12" x 18" black construction paper, glue, tape (optional), self-adhesive stars or yellow or white crayon, paper fastener (optional)

Directions: Copy and cut out the world reproducible. Color the land and water areas with green and blue crayons or markers, respectively. Glue the cutout vertically in the center of the black construction paper. *Note:* If you want to have a spinning globe like the one in the "We Care for Mother Earth" bulletin board, instead of gluing, poke a hole in the center of the globe and the black paper, slip in a paper fastener, and secure on the back.

Trace the child's hands (fingers apart) on a sheet of skin-tone construction paper. Cut out the paper hands. Tape or glue each hand so that the fingers point upward and touch the world (or almost touch it in the case of a "spinning" world). Add self-adhesive stars (or hand-drawn ones in white or yellow crayon) to the black "outer space" background. Presto! The child has the whole, wide world in his or her hands!

"Hand-y" Flower Holder

Children will have these special flower holders long after the project is over to remind them that caring for Mother Earth is a year-long job. And even though the flower is silk, it's representative of the natural resources we need to protect.

Materials: Poster board, scissors, crayons or markers (brown, green, dark blue, tan or orange, light blue), stapler and staples, small silk flower, transparent tape, pencil

Directions: Trace the child's hands (fingers apart) on the poster board. Color each thumb and finger on both hands with a color that represents a natural resource, for example: green—forest, brown—earth, dark blue—water, tan or orange—sand, light blue—sky. Print the name of each resource below the finger or thumb in the palm area. Cut out the poster board hands and staple the palm areas together so that the colored side of each hand shows. Then tape a silk flower between the two thumbs and tape closed. The child may take this project home and share its "Embracing the Earth" lessons with someone he or she loves.

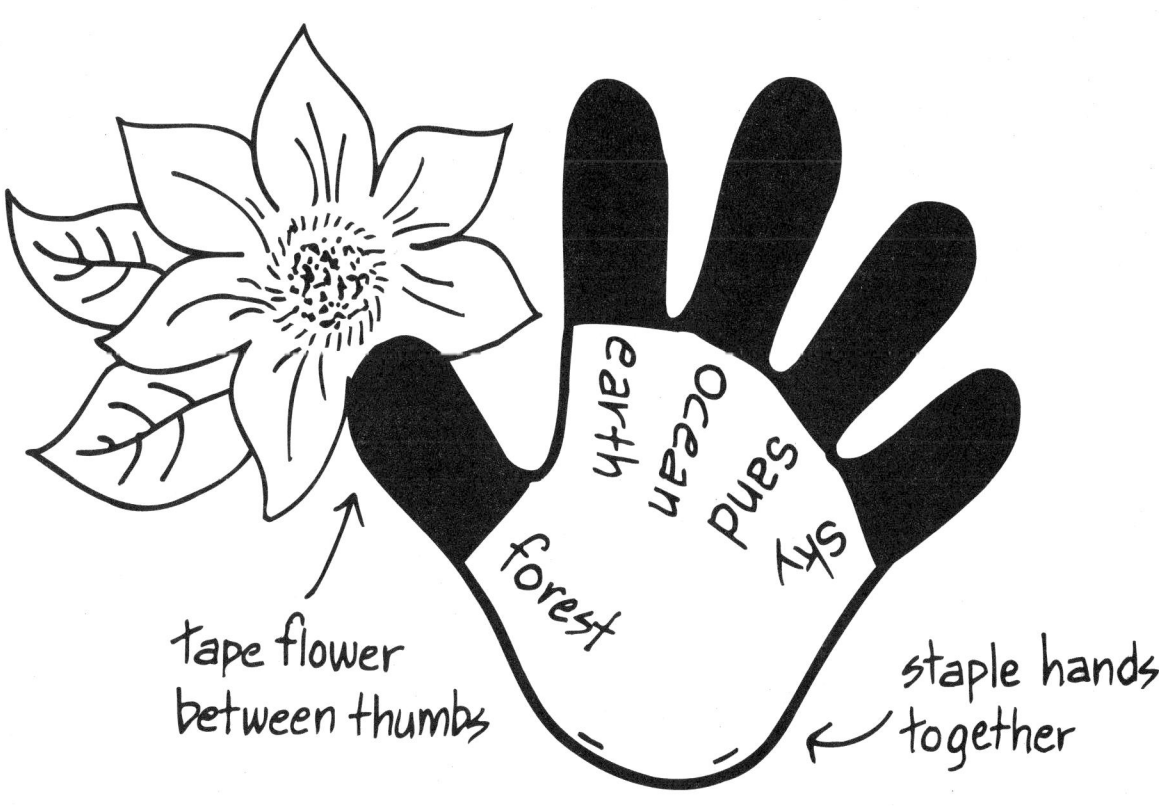

Embracing the Earth Finger Plays and Movement Songs

Oh, Apple Tree
(to the tune of "O Christmas Tree")

Oh, apple tree, oh, apple tree,
We love to climb your branches!
Oh, apple tree, oh, apple tree,
We love to climb your branches!

The apples grow so red and ripe,
When they're picked we take a bite.
And all who rest from summer's sun
Sit cool in shade when work is done.

Hush, Little Children
(to the tune of "Hush, Little Baby")

Hush, little children, don't you cry.
Mama washes jars and lets them dry.
When they're dry, Mama has a bin
That all recyclable stuff goes in.

Then a man in a truck pulls up
And loads those jars in his great big truck.
Mama says she feels extra fine
When she helps the Earth live a long, long time!

Home Is Our Earth
(to the tune of "Home on the Range")

Home, home is our Earth,
Where the children and animals play.
Where seldom is heard
A wasteful word,
We reuse and recycle all day!

Home, home is our Earth,
And we're proud to be caring for her.
We love all her trees,
The birds and the bees,
And the sky unpolluted all day!

Embracing the Earth Read-Alouds

Fiction

Blos, Joan. *It's Spring She Said.* New York: Knopf, 1968.

Funny pictures by Julie Maas; kids will love this book.

Cole, Joanna. *The Magic School Bus at the Waterworks.* New York: Scholastic, 1986.

Ms. Frizzle the teacher certainly is made up, but all the information she presents to her students about waterworks is the real thing. Wonderful comic book-style illustrations. Also by the author: *The Magic School Bus Inside the Earth*, with great information about soil and fossils.

Cooney, Barbara. *Miss Rumphius.* New York: Viking, 1982.

The Lupine Lady is little and old, but her mission to make the world a prettier place began when she was just a little girl. Wonderfully illustrated by a master storyteller.

Fleischman, Paul. *Joyful Noise—Poems for Two Voices.* New York: The Trumpet Club, 1988.

Insects from grasshoppers to fireflies to moths to honeybees are included in these delightful poems.

Frost, Robert. *Stopping by Woods on a Snowy Evening.* New York: Dutton, 1969.

Robert Frost's treasured poem comes alive for preschoolers in wonderful pictures by Susan Jeffers. Many of the illustrations were inspired by the woods outside the artist's studio.

Hallinan, P.K. *For the Love of Our Earth.* Nashville, Tenn.: Ideals, 1992.

This is one of the best picture books for teaching young children about ecology, because they relate to the words and pictures. Paperback versions are available from Ideals Publishing Corporation, Nashville, TN 37210.

Kellogg, Steven. *Johnny Appleseed.* New York: Scholastic, 1988.

Legend comes alive for young children in this simplified story of John Chapman—the boy who loved apple trees.

Morrison, Meeghan. *Long Live Earth.* New York: Scholastic, 1993.

Lovely illustrations teach preschoolers about caring for Mother Earth.

Ryder, Joanne. *Hello, Tree.* New York: Lodestar, 1991.

Tall oaks line the century-old streets in historic Oak Park, Illinois, but children don't have to live there to appreciate the value of this picture book. Beautifully illustrated by Michael Hays.

Wildsmith, Brian. *Professor Noah's Spaceship.* Oxford: Oxford University Press, 1980.

The animals in the forest are concerned that their environment is too polluted and can't support them any more. Professor Noah has a solution, but can the animals reach their destination in time to save themselves?

Nonfiction

Ehlert, Lois. *Red Leaf, Yellow Leaf.* New York: Harcourt Brace, 1991.

Lois Ehlert is a master storyteller and illustrator who presents information in such a wonderful way that even young children relate to it.

Heller, Ruth. *Plants That Never Ever Bloom.* New York: Scholastic, 1984.

Plants come in all sizes and grow in many different places.

Jordan, Helene J. *How a Seed Grows.* New York: Crowell, 1960.

Very practical information that young children can understand.

Kirkpatrick, Rena. *Look at Flowers.* Milwaukee, Wisc.: Raintree, 1978.

Children can learn the names of flowers in this helpful resource.

Siebert, Diane. *Heartland.* New York: Crowell, 1989.

Anyone who has ever lived in or traveled through the Midwest can relate to the wonderfully realistic illustrations by Wendell Minor. Very appropriate for this unit since America's heartland provides much of the food for the entire nation.

Wilkes, Angela. *My First Nature Book.* New York: Knopf, 1990.

Beautifully illustrated with "seeing is touching" photos. Step-by-step directions teach children to plant and collect seeds and make a showcase among many other projects.

Yolen, Jane. *Welcome to the Green House.* New York: Scholastic, 1993.

With this book you can take young children into nature's hothouse where the sun bursts through a canopy of leaves. Illustrated by Laura Regan, who helps make the trip to the tropical rain forest very real.

Embracing the Earth Snacktime

Flower Pot Dessert

This creation looks great to kids—and it tastes great too!

Ingredients: 2 small packages of instant vanilla pudding mix, 3 cups milk, 8 oz. cream cheese, 1 stick butter or margarine, 12 oz. Cool Whip, 1 1/4 lb. package of Oreo cookies, mixing bowls, 8" clay flower pot, foil, silk or plastic flowers

Directions: Stir together the vanilla pudding mixes and the milk. In a separate bowl, mix together the cream cheese (softened) and the butter or margarine (softened). Add the pudding mixture and mix together. Then add the Cool Whip (thawed) and mix well. Crush the Oreo cookies.

To assemble this treat, line the flower pot with foil. Pour in some of the pudding mixture. Place some of the crushed Oreos on top for "dirt." Continue layering the pudding mixture and the cookie bits. Then wrap silk or plastic flower stems in foil and stick in the middle of the dessert. After the pudding has set and the children have admired the creation,

Embracing the Earth Games

Mother Earth Toss

All you need is a big, soft ball to play this game—blue or green if possible to represent the Earth. (An inflatable "globe" ball would be great too.) Just have the children toss the ball back and forth while music plays. When you stop the music, whoever has the ball tells one way he or she takes care of Mother Earth. Record all the responses on a big poster that can be displayed as an Earth-friendly reminder.

Note: Young children will need to be given some answers before playing the game. Examples: I pick up toys, I put my fruit drink containers in the trash, I help my mom and dad recycle plastic.

Flip-Your-Lid Match

Save those metal lids from frozen juice containers for this matching game! (Other lids work too, but be sure they don't have sharp edges.)

Materials: Metal lids, Earth-theme self-adhesive stickers (trees, animals, Earth, flowers; two of each design)

Directions: Fasten one sticker of each pair to one side of a lid. Line up the lids in rows (horizontally and vertically). Then mix up the lids so that matching stickers aren't next to each other. Flip the lids over so the stickers aren't showing. Then have the children play "Concentration," trying to remember where the matching stickers are located. When a match is made, the child takes the paired lids and sets them aside. Start a new game when all the lids have been matched and taken out of play.

HONORING EXPLORERS

Trying out new ideas, discovering new lands, reaching to the sky—explorers capture our interest as they stretch for new worlds just beyond the horizon. While there could be an entire *BodyArt* book on the wonders explorers have brought to us, this unit focuses on three important firsts: Columbus's discovery of the New World, the Wright brothers' invention of the airplane, and Neil Armstrong and Buzz Aldrin's landing on the moon.

To honor Christopher Columbus, certainly one of the most famous explorers, children will be recreating the ship he navigated across the ocean, the *Santa Maria*. They'll also be putting together a *BodyArt* replica of the Wright brothers' first airplane, flown in 1903. Finally, they'll move through time and space with their very own rocket—and then step on the moon!

Encourage children to let their imaginations soar as they create and learn in this exciting unit. After all, they're part of the next generation of great explorers!

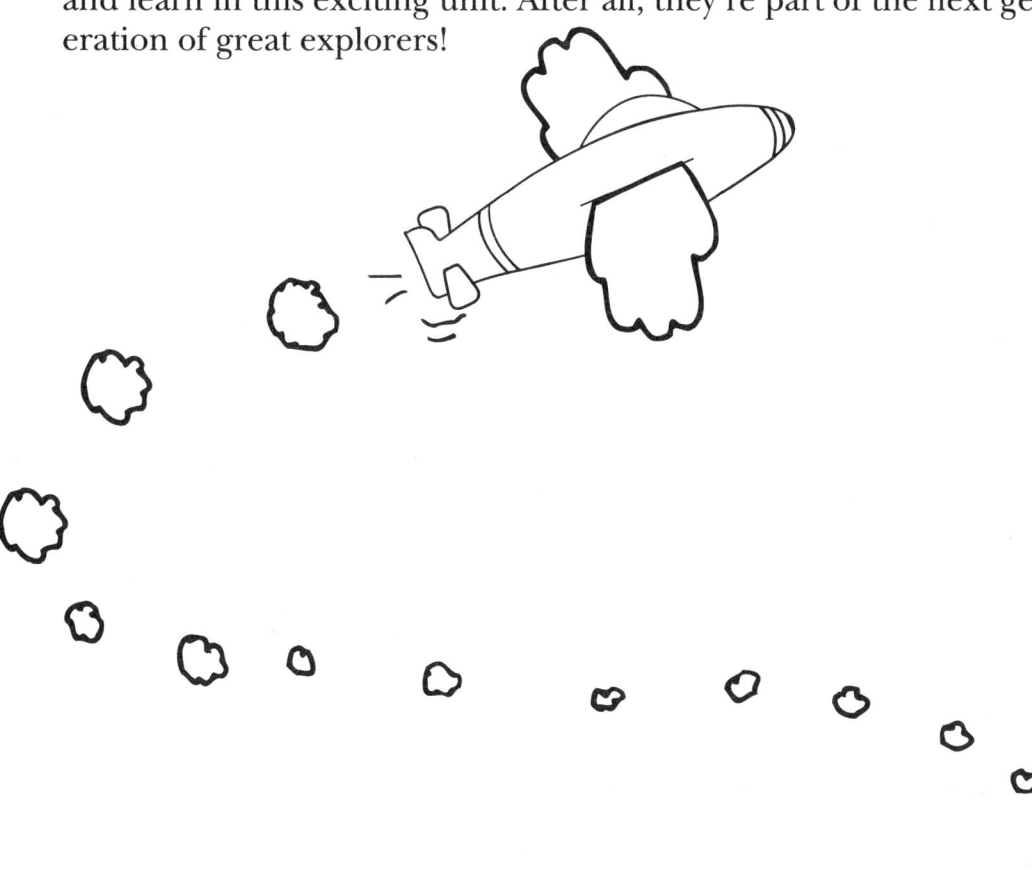

Moving Through Time and Space Bulletin Board

Capture the explorer's adventurous spirit in this bulletin board time line—Columbus's ship comes first, then the Wright brothers' plane, and finally a rocket to the moon!

Materials: White poster board; marker; construction paper (blue, green, white, black); tape; glue; scissors; silver glitter; copies of the completed ship, airplane, and rocket and moon projects (pp. 35-37)

Directions: Each of the three projects will take up one-third of the bulletin board. Columbus's ship will be at the far left. The Wright brothers' plane will go in the center, and the rocket will be last.

To make the "ocean" background for the *Santa Maria*, cut two wavy shapes from blue construction paper. Position on the poster board, then tape or glue down the edges and puff out the center to give the "waves" a three-dimensional look. Tape or glue the *Santa Maria* atop one of the waves.

In the center, glue a sheet of blue construction paper vertically to represent the sky for the plane. Glue a sheet of green paper beneath the blue one to represent a grassy field. Add clouds by tracing the child's hands (fingers together) on white paper. Cut out the hands and glue to the sky. Glue or tape the airplane below the clouds.

The right side of the bulletin board is for a sparkling moon landing. Glue white star shapes to a sheet of black construction paper. Add a bit more glue and sprinkle on silver glitter. Dust off excess glitter. When the glue had dried, glue the completed "outer space" background vertically to the right side of the board. Glue or tape on the completed moon and rocket.

The Santa Maria

The *Santa Maria* was the largest of the three ships that headed for the New World with Christopher Columbus. The ship was captained by Columbus, a European mapmaker who thought he could sail west instead of east to reach China and Japan, home of precious spices and silk. On October 12, 1492, Columbus and his ships landed at what is now called Watling Island in the Bahamas, off the coast of America.

Materials: Ship reproducible (p. 41), scissors, brown crayon or marker, white bond paper, transparent tape, pencil, nontoxic glue, 12" x 18" white construction paper, 8 ½" x 10" blue construction paper

Directions: Copy, color, and cut out the ship reproducible. Trace the child's hand (fingers together) on a sheet of white bond paper. Cut out the paper hand and set aside. Glue the ship to a sheet of white construction paper positioned vertically. Cut out wave shapes from blue construction paper and tape to the white construction paper below the ship; tape the edges of the waves so the center puffs out for a three-dimensional look. Attach the white paper hand to the *Santa Maria* for a sail by centering the sail over the ship and then taping or gluing down the base of the hand. Fold the rest of the paper hand back and forth into a soft accordion shape before gluing down the top of the hand. Let the ship sail home with the explorer at unit's end!

Wild Blue Yonder Flying

On December 17, 1903, Orville Wright piloted the first powered airplane flight, in Kitty Hawk, North Carolina. Later that day, Wilbur Wright flew a second flight of 852 feet. Your children can join in the Wrights' adventures by making their own *BodyArt* airplane.

Materials: Plane reproducible (p. 42), silver (or other-colored) crayon, scissors, pencil, white poster board, 8 1/2" x 10" construction paper (blue, green, white), nontoxic glue, hole punch (optional), picture wire (optional), Velcro (optional)

Directions: Copy, color, and cut out the plane reproducible. Cut a slit where indicated. Make wings by tracing the child's hands on a piece of white poster board. Color the "wings" silver and cut out. Glue the heels of the wings together. When dry, slide the paper wings through the slit. To make a background for the plane, follow the directions for the airplane section of the bulletin board (p. 34). Attach a small piece of Velcro to the background and to the plane so that the plane can "take off" and "land." Or punch a hole in the plane and add a length of picture wire for hanging.

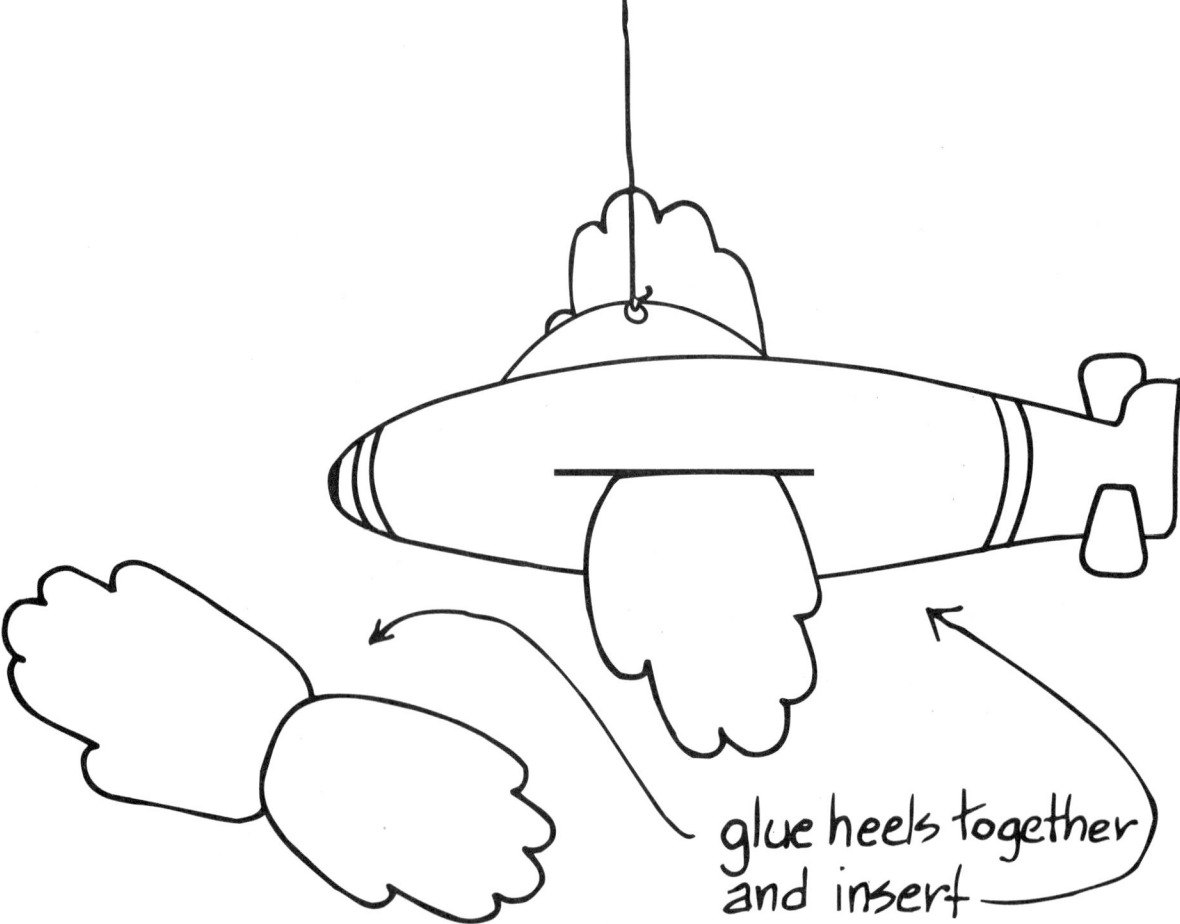

glue heels together and insert

Moon Stepping

On July 20, 1969, Neil Armstrong and Edwin "Buzz" Aldrin stepped out of their lunar lander and fulfilled man's ancient dream of taking a voyage to the moon. Now your children can see their own footsteps on the moon!

Materials: Moon and rocket reproducibles (pp. 43-44), nontoxic glue, brush, hole punch, scissors, white poster board, paper fastener, crayons (black, red, blue), silver glitter, marker, transparent tape

Directions: Trace the child's feet on a piece of white poster board. Using the moon reproducible as a guide, cut out the white poster board in the same moon shape. Add the words "I stepped on the moon!" below the foot tracings and the child's name in one of the foot outlines. Set the poster board aside.

Color the moon reproducible black. Brush on spots of glue and add silver glitter. (Make sure glitter stays out of the child's eyes.) Brush off excess glue. Then copy, color, and cut out the rocket ship. Glue the rocket ship to the moon and let dry completely.

Next, position the poster board with the child's foot tracings (toes should be pointing up) beneath the moon reproducible. Trim the poster board if necessary so that it matches the moon shape. Punch a hole in the top center of both moon reproducible and white poster board. Insert a paper fastener through both pieces and secure at the back. Now the child can swing the moon up to reveal his or her footsteps!

Honoring Explorers Finger Plays and Movement Songs

The Explorers' Song
(to the tune of "The Farmer in the Dell")

Columbus discovered new land,
Columbus discovered new land,
High-ho the derry-o,
Columbus discovered new land!

The Wright brothers learned to fly,
The Wright brothers learned to fly,
High-ho the derry-o,
The Wright brothers learned to fly!

Armstrong walked on the moon,
Aldrin walked on the moon,
High-ho the derry-o,
Two men walked on the moon!

The Astronaut Song
(to the tune of "Ten Little Indians")

One brave, two brave, three brave astronauts,
Four brave, five brave, six brave astronauts,
Seven brave, eight brave, nine brave astronauts,
Ten brave astronauts all!

Moon Stepping
(to the tune of "The Hokey Pokey"—do the movements slowly)

You put your moon foot in,
You put your moon foot out,
You put your moon foot in
And shake it all about.
You moon step here and you moon step there.
That's what it's all about!

(Continue, substituting other body parts: moon arm, moon fingers, moon head, etc.)

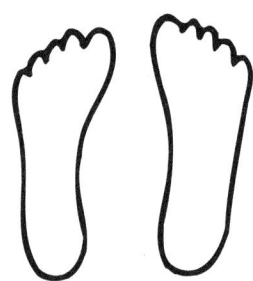

Honoring Explorers Read-Alouds

Fiction

Asch, Frank. *Mooncake*. New York: Prentice-Hall, 1983.

One evening Bear tells Little Bird that he'd like to take a bite out of the moon. Soon he falls asleep in a homemade rocket. When he wakes up, it's winter. Bear eats snow and thinks it's a mooncake!

Cole, Joanna. *The Magic School Bus—Lost in the Solar System*. New York: Scholastic, 1990.

Ms. Frizzle's at it again! She'll stop at nothing to get her class interested in the solar system—even if it means taking a field trip to outer space! More exploration takes place in the *Magic School Bus on the Ocean Floor*.

Marshall, Edward. *Space Case*. New York: Dial, 1980.

An outer-spaceman finds happiness and friendship when he joins Earthly trick-or-treaters on Halloween. A "Reading Rainbow" featured offering.

McPhail, David. *The Dream Child*. New York: Dutton, 1985.

This beautifully illustrated picture book tells about Dream Child and the journey she and her stuffed bear take when the moon rises.

Spier, Peter. *Bored—Nothing to Do!* New York: Trumpet Club, 1978.

There's never a boring moment when two brothers have lots of materials and great imagination. Why, they might even fly their own homemade plane just like another famous brother team did!

Udry, Janice May. *The Moon Jumpers*. New York: Trumpet Club, 1959.

Maurice Sendak's illustrations and Janice May Udry's story capture the glorious feeling of playing with friends in summer moonlight.

Wildsmith, Brian. *What the Moon Saw*. Oxford: Oxford University Press, 1978.

Moon tells Sun she wants to see more of the world, so Sun tells Moon about such things as big and little, inside and outside.

Willard, Nancy. *The Nightgown of the Sullen Moon*. San Diego, Calif.: Harcourt Brace, 1983.

Moon loves her blue flannel nightgown stitched with stars. Unfortunately she can't shine when she wears it.

Nonfiction

Cavendish, Marshall. *Children of History: Wilbur & Orville Wright*. New York: Rowland-Entwistle-Theodore, 1988.

A special read-to about the famous brothers who began the Air Age.

Lepscky, Ibi. *Leonardo da Vinci*. New York: Trumpet Club, 1984.

Leonardo's curiosity leads him to create all sorts of famous firsts. He even made drawings of a flying machine!

Maestro, Betsy and Giulio. *The Discovery of the Americas*. New York: Scholastic, 1991.

A read-to book that may be a bit difficult for young listeners, but they'll be interested in the pictures.

Honoring Explorers Snacktime

Moon Pies!

If you live in the South, a Moon Pie is a perfect treat to offer during this unit. But wherever you live, Moon Pie equivalents called S'mores will be welcome (and you don't need a campfire to make them).

Ingredients: Graham cracker squares, thin bars of chocolate, marshmallow spread

Directions: Coat one side of a graham cracker square with marshmallow spread right from the jar. Break off pieces of the candy bar and layer them on. Top the sweets with another graham cracker square and squeeze together lightly. Then enjoy a taste that sends you to the moon!

Honoring Explorers Game

Slo-Mo Dancing

This fun game is played like the game "Statues," but children play it in slow motion—just the way the astronauts walked on the moon!

Show children how to move slowwwwwly! Let them practice a while. Then put on some music (Raffi songs work well) and let the children moon-walk to it. Stop the music occasionally and have the children "freeze" in place. Continue playing while interest remains high.

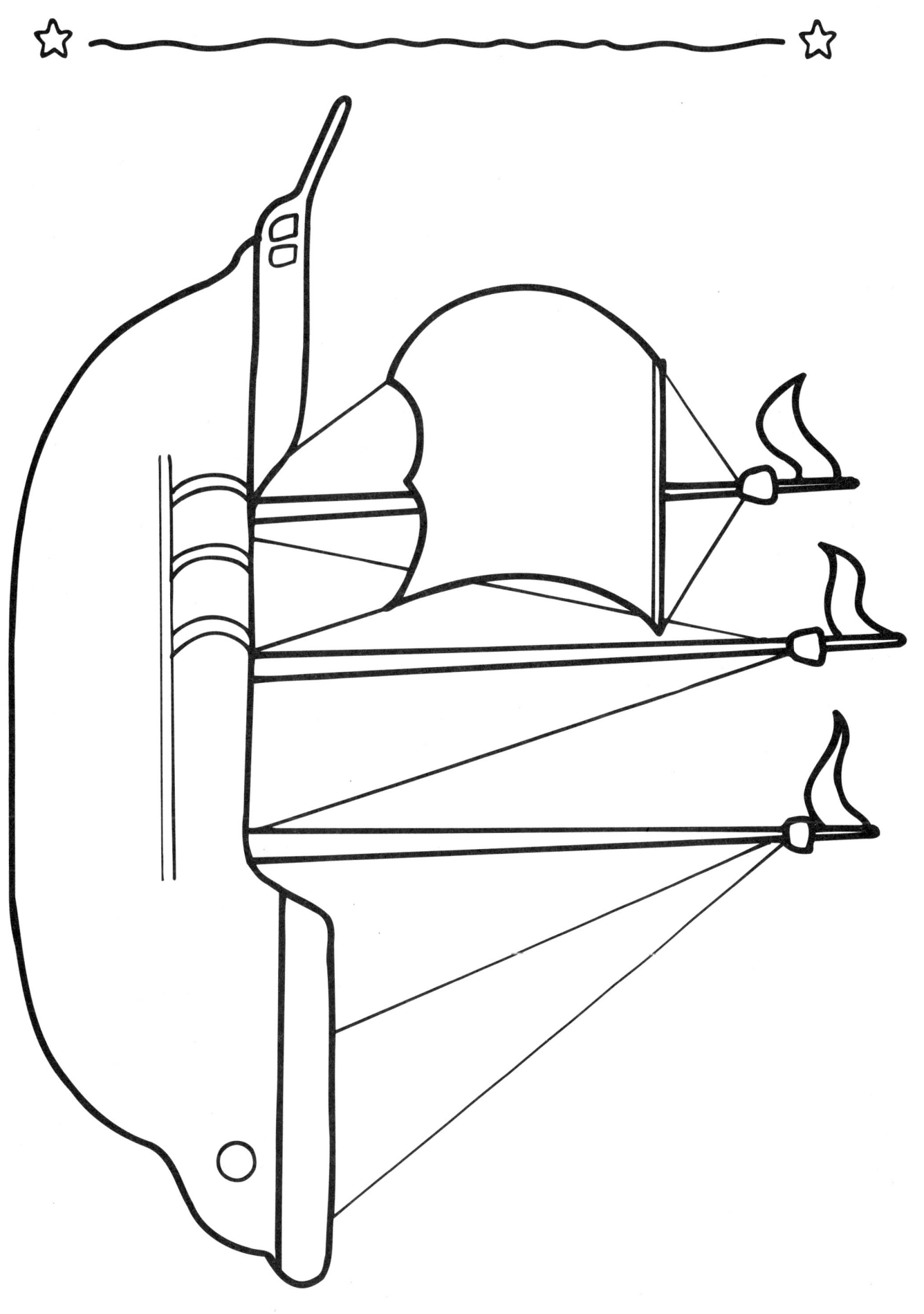

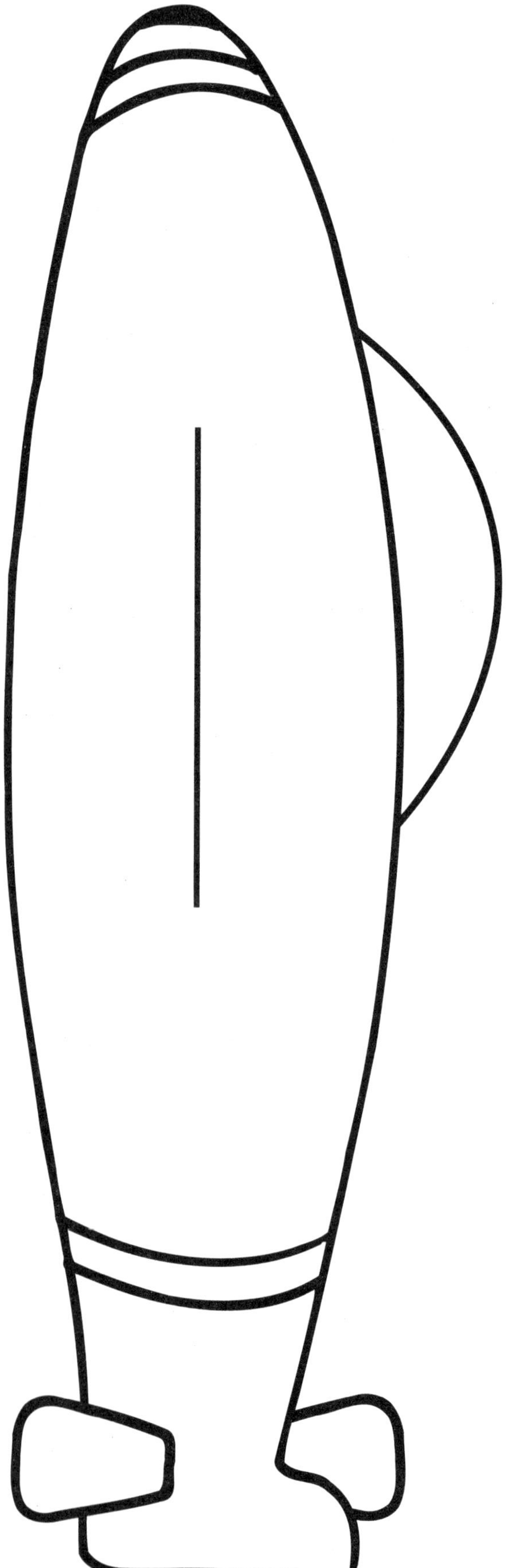

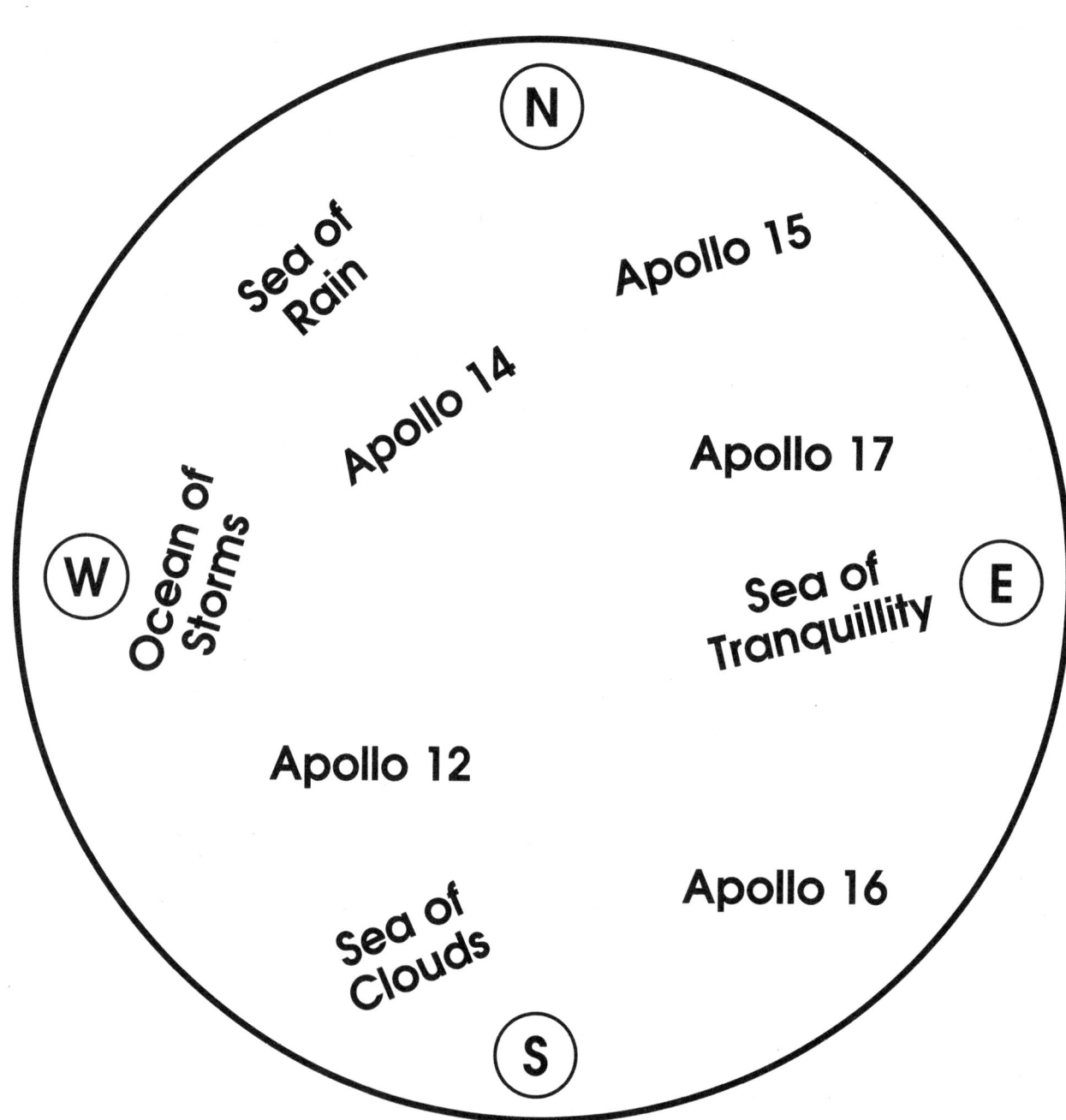

LET'S HEAR IT FOR LEADERS!

A good leader is someone who responsibly guides or leads others in a direction that will help make the world a better place. George Washington, for example, was asked if he wanted to be king of the newly independent United States. He said he'd rather be elected to lead by the people. As a result, he became the new nation's first president, and included citizens in the governing process.

Another president, Abraham Lincoln, fought to end slavery in the United States. He also worked hard to keep the states united as one nation. Had he lived, the nation's wounds from the Civil War might have healed much faster.

Like Lincoln, Martin Luther King, Jr., died before he could do all the things he wanted to do. He dedicated his life to making sure black Americans were treated the same as other citizens. His ideas are remembered because he was a good leader who believed equality could be achieved without the use of violence.

Women have also provided leadership. Harriet Tubman (1820-1913) is not only considered one of the first black American activists, but her role as founder of the Underground Railroad earned her the title "Moses of the People." Thanks to her effort, many slaves were channeled into free states via this elaborate secret network.

Moms, dads, step-parents, grandparents, and teachers also are honored in this unit. These nurturing adults are perhaps the most important people in young children's lives. Their guidance and direction will set the tone for what leadership is all about.

Follow the Leader Bulletin Board

Now children can follow in the footsteps of famous leaders with this bulletin board that incorporates the foot as part of the design.

Materials: Pencil, markers or crayons, construction paper, scissors, glue, white poster board, masking tape

Directions: Trace each child's foot on a sheet of construction paper. Cut out the paper feet. These will be the faces of the leaders you want to display. Use markers or crayons to add facial features and hair to the faces. Some leaders will look more natural with the paper heel on top; others will look better with the paper toes on top. Experiment with the list of leaders in the song on page 51 to see what works for you. Glue the completed leaders on a large sheet of white poster board, leaving several spaces in the bottom right row so that children can add their care givers' faces. Then print the name of each leader below each paper foot.

Repeat the steps for paper feet representations of the children's care givers. Attach them in the empty spaces on the bulletin board with small, rolled pieces of masking tape.

Washington's Cherry Tree

Did George Washington really chop down the family cherry tree when he was a boy? It may just be a story, but the point makes a good lesson for children everywhere: always tell the truth.

Materials: White, heavy cardboard; ruler; utility knife; scissors; brushes; paint trays; nontoxic, washable red, brown, and green tempera paint; markers

Directions: Before introducing this activity, have an adult prepare undecorated trees ahead of time. First, draw an 8 ½" x 11" summer-foliage tree (with lots of billowy leaves) on cardboard and cut out. Use this as a template for making a second tree. The trees should be the same size so that they can be easily joined to make one three-dimensional tree.

Using a scissors or utility knife, cut a vertical slit in the top center of one of the cardboard trees. Extend the slit straight down, ending three inches from the bottom. On the second cardboard tree, make a cut in the bottom center and extend straight upward, stopping two inches from the top. Use a ruler to guide your cutting lines. Then slip both cardboard pieces into each other and see if they will stand. Adjust your slits if they don't. Take the trees apart.

Now have the child paint both sides of the cardboard trees. Encourage brushing on a thin coat of brown paint for the trunk and a thin coat of green for the leaves; this will help the trees dry faster. After the paint has dried, the child can dip finger tips into a tray of red paint and add cherries to the tree. After all the paint is dry, have an adult join the two cardboard trees to make one.

slip cardboard pieces into each other

Lincoln's Beard

Abraham Lincoln was a tall, thin man with hollow cheeks and a sad expression. His appearance led one young girl to write to him urging him to grow a beard so his face would look better! Lincoln took her advice and grew a beard, and he never shaved it off.

Materials: Fake fur; scissors; Velcro; pencil; white poster board; non-toxic, washable markers or crayons; paper fastener; black construction paper; fabric scraps (optional)

Directions: Trace the child's foot on a piece of poster board. Cut out the paper foot "face." Position the paper foot so that the heel is Honest Abe's chin and the toes are the top of his head. Color in hair and facial features with markers or crayons. Cut out a black construction paper top hat using the width of the paper toe area to size the hat's brim. Attach the hat to the top of Lincoln's head with a paper fastener. Position the fastener to one side so that the hat can be tipped up or down on Lincoln's head.

To make Lincoln's beard, trace the child's hand (fingers together) on the back of a piece of fake fur. Have an adult cut out the hand shape. Attach the beard to Lincoln's chin with Velcro. For more fun, make additional beards. Trace the child's hands (fingers together) on fabric scraps and cut out. Attach the silly fabric beards with Velcro. Let the child have fun moving Lincoln's hat up and down and putting on the variety of beards.

Soar Like an Eagle!

What better symbol of leadership than the magnificent bald eagle!

Materials: Eagle reproducible (p. 54), scissors, brown crayon or marker, brown construction paper, wooden craft stick, glue, poster board or cardboard, transparent tape, pencil, paper fastener

Directions: Copy the eagle reproducible and color in the body with brown marker or crayon (leave the head white). Cut out and glue a piece of cardboard or poster board to the back for extra strength and durability. Trace the child's hands (fingers together) on a sheet of brown construction paper. Cut out both paper hands. Fold the "wings" lengthwise and position so that one wing has fingers pointing up and the other has fingers pointing down. Overlap the heel ends of the hands by 1/2". Then position the hands in the center of the eagle's body. Punch a hole through the two wings and the body and secure with a paper fastener. Put a piece of transparent tape over any rough edges. Tape a wooden craft stick to the back of the eagle's body and let the child soar with the soaring *BodyArt* eagle!

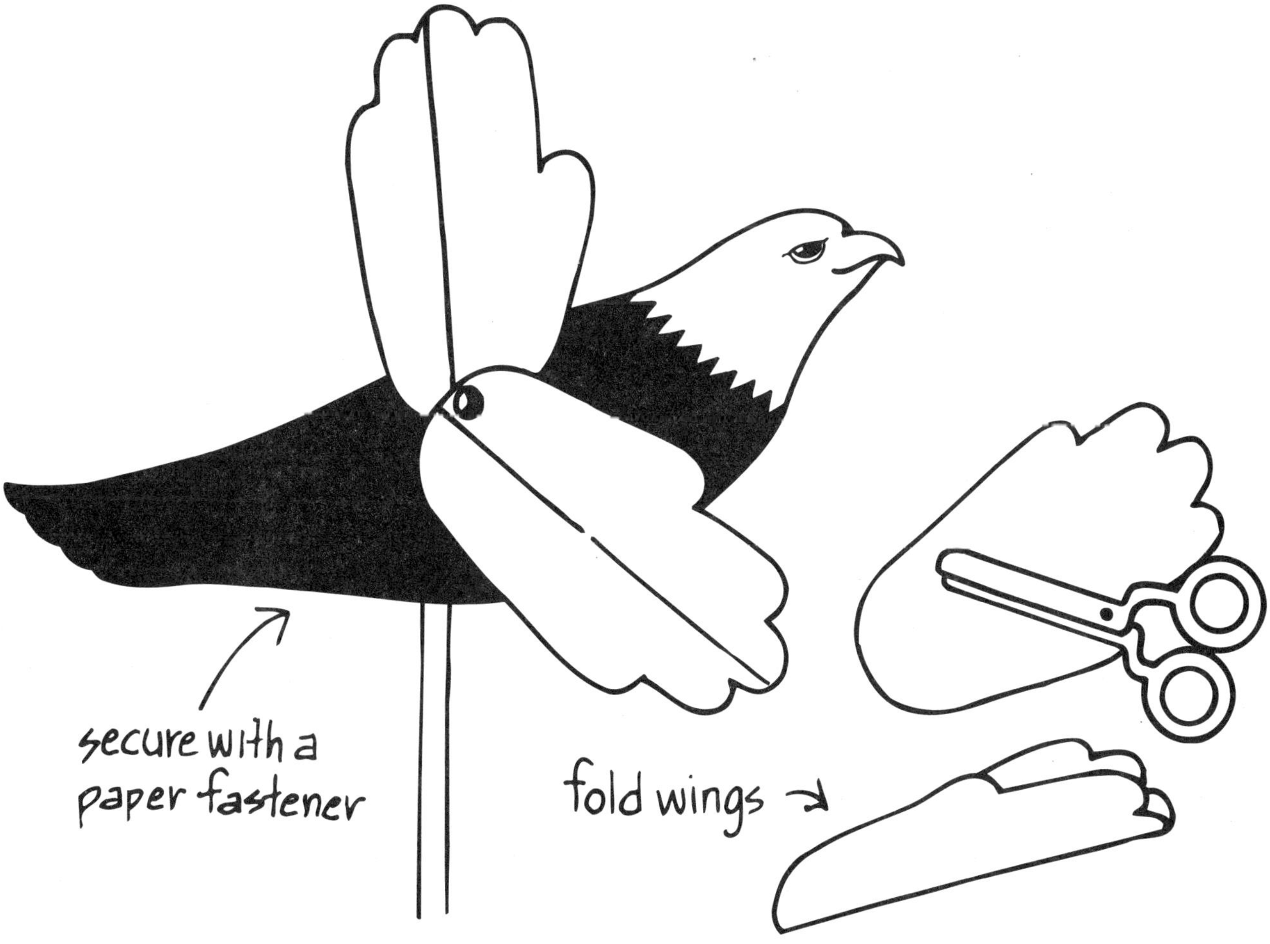

secure with a paper fastener

fold wings

Helping Hands

Helping hands make leaders responsible people. Even young children can help out around the house by picking up their toys.

Materials: Hole punch, 7 colors of construction paper, paper fastener, scissors, pencil, thin-tipped marker

Directions: Trace the child's hand on a sheet of construction paper. Repeat six more times on different colors of paper. Cut out the paper hands and punch a hole in the heel portion of each one. Join the seven hands with a paper fastener. Have an adult print a "helping hands" job title on each hand for the week. Examples: Quick Toy Picker Upper, Famous Family Pet Feeder, Quick Clothes Picker Upper, Terrific Teeth Brusher, Awesome Hair Comber.

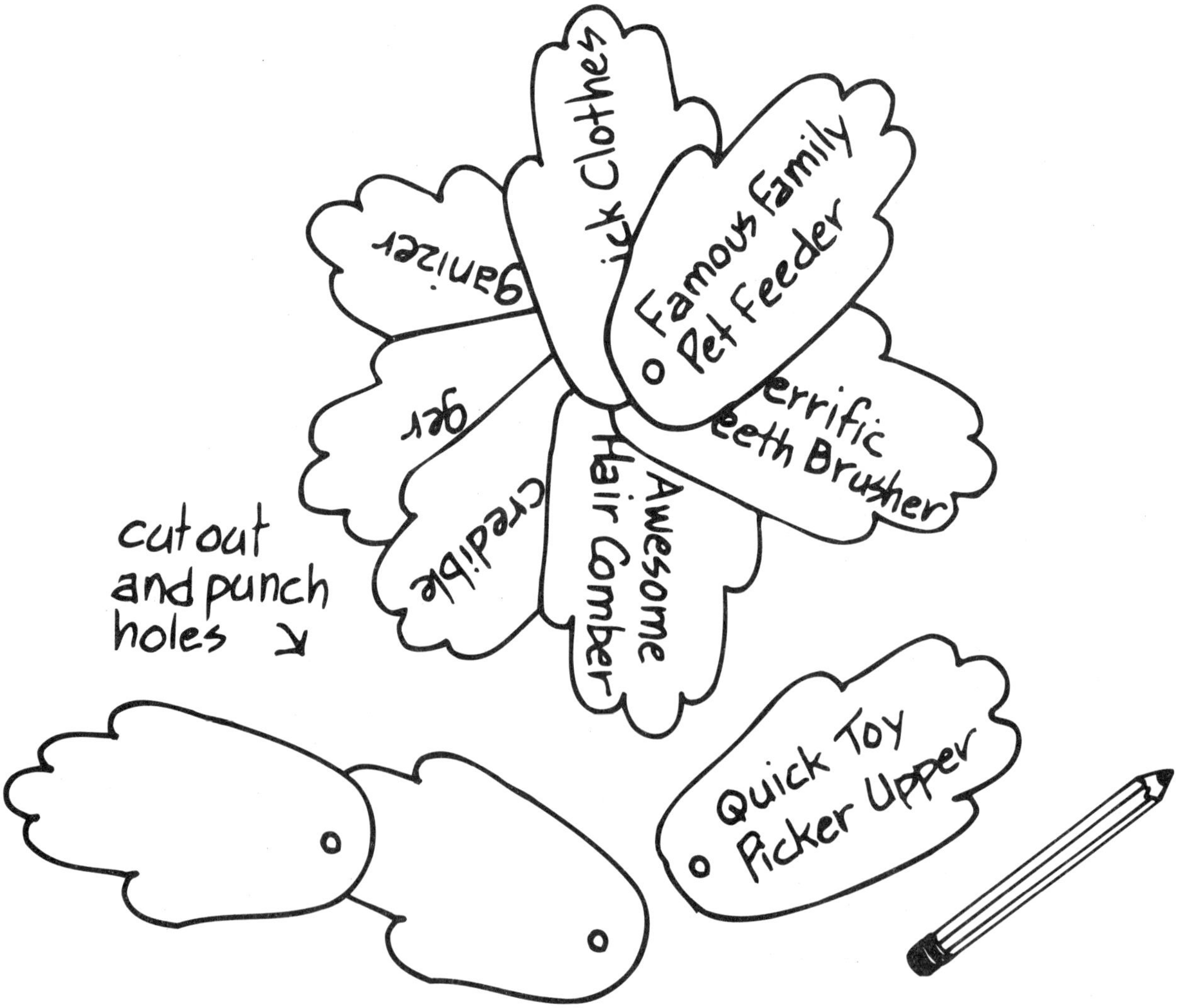

cut out and punch holes

Let's Hear It for Leaders Finger Plays and Movement Songs

How to Get Rid of Monsters Song

(to the tune of "The Bear Went Over the Mountain")

The leader went over the mountain,
The leader went over the mountain,
The leader went over the mountain
To see what he could see.

He saw a great big monster!
He saw a great big monster!
He saw a great big monster!
'Twas all that he could see.

I have to save the village!
I have to save the village!
I have to save the village!
That's what the leader said.

He gave the monster some pepper!
He gave the monster some pepper!
He gave the monster some pepper!
Then he sat back and watched.

The monster sneezed and sneezed!
The monster sneezed and sneezed!
The monster sneezed and sneezed
And was never seen again!

The Silly Leader Song

(to the tune of "Hail, Hail, the Gang's All Here")

Hail, hail, the leader's here.
What's he going to tell us?
What's he going to tell us?
Hail, hail, the leader's here.
Now he says to hop around!

Hail, hail, the leader's here.
What's she going to tell us?
What's she going to tell us?
Hail, hail, the leader's here.
Now she says to touch our toes!

Hail, hail, the leader's here.
Where's he going to lead us?
Where's he going to lead us?
Hail, hail, the leader's here.
He says to go in and out!

Hail, hail, the leader's here.
Where's she going to lead us?
Where's she going to lead us?
Hail, hail, the leader's here.
She says run in circles now!

(Add or change verses as you like and let children act out the last line of each one.)

Leader Cheer

Two, four, six, eight,
Who do we appreciate?
_____!

(Fill in the name of a leader, such as Dr. Martin Luther King, Sally Ride, Ben Franklin, Harriet Tubman, Abraham Lincoln, George Washington, Mom, Dad, Grandma, Grandpa. If names don't fit the rhythm of the cheer, repeat the first name and use the last name once only. Example: Florence, Florence, Florence Nightingale!)

End with: Leaders, leaders, leaders all!

Let's Hear It for Leaders Read-Alouds

Fiction

Carlstrom, Nancy White. *Grandpappy.* Boston: Little, Brown, 1990.

Special times between a boy and his grandfather are detailed in this lovely book.

Fritz, Jean. *George Washington's Breakfast.* New York: Trumpet Club, 1969.

Illustrator Paul Galdone joins forces with storyteller extraordinaire Jean Fritz in this wonderful story about how George W. Allen is proud that his birthday is the same as George Washington's.

Fritz, Jean. *What's the Big Idea, Ben Franklin?* New York: Coward-McCann, 1976.

Ben Franklin was always coming up with great ideas—from a circulating library to electricity. This excellent read-to helps explain who Ben Franklin was to young readers.

Hallinan, P.K. *My Father and I.* Nashville, Tenn.: Ideals, 1989.

One of a series of books that explores special relationships between children and the important people in their lives. Other titles include *My Mother and I, Grandpa and I, My Brother and I, My Sister and I, That's What a Friend Is For.*

Quinlan, Patricia. *My Dad Takes Care of Me.* Ontario, Canada: Annick Press, 1987.

Mr. Mom shares special times with his son in addition to going to school to learn new career skills; Mom has a 9-to-5 computer-related job.

Thayer, Ernest Lawrence. *Casey at the Bat.* New York: Dover, 1977.

The ballad about the famous baseball player is recreated here for young readers. There are black and white illustrations by Jim Hull and a detailed introduction by Martin Gardner.

Yolen, Jane. *Owl Moon.* New York: Philomel, 1987.

Simple rituals often bond parents and children together. In this family, owling is such a ritual, and dad turns it into a very important lesson in hope. A Caldecott Medal winner featured on PBS's "Reading Rainbow."

Nonfiction

Ancona, George. *Helping Out.* New York: Clarion, 1985.

Striking photographs and easy-to-read sentences show the many ways children can lend a hand with grown-up tasks. These include handing someone else a tool and more involving chores such as washing the car.

Marzollo, Jean. *Happy Birthday, Martin Luther King.* New York: Scholastic, 1993.

This preschool paperback tells about Dr. King's leadership capabilities through sensitively written text and lovely pictures.

Raynor, Dorka. *Grandparents Around the World.* Chicago: Albert Whitman, 1977.

Black and white photographs portray the global nature of the love shared between grandchildren and their grandparents.

Let's Hear It for Leaders Snacktime

The Hero Sandwich

Good leaders are heroes! Celebrate the wonderful lessons leaders have taught us by making (and devouring!) a hero sandwich. (In some areas hero sandwiches are called submarines.)

Slice a loaf of Italian bread (the longer, the better) down the middle and spread with mayonnaise and mustard. Layer on all the children's favorites: lettuce, cheese, salami, chicken, beef, tomatoes—the choice is theirs! The bigger the sandwich, the better! Hand out individual slices with plenty of napkins.

Let's Hear It for Leaders Game

Follow the Leader

A traditional but still wonderful game for learning about leadership!

Directions: Select one child to be the leader and have him or her stand in front of the other children. Everyone must do what the leader does. Limit the time to a minute or two, and then change children until everyone has had a chance to lead. To make their time as leader fun, suggest children do such things as touch toes, do jumping jacks, skip, hop, pat their head, bend to one side, make a funny face, shake hands with someone else, and clap their hands.

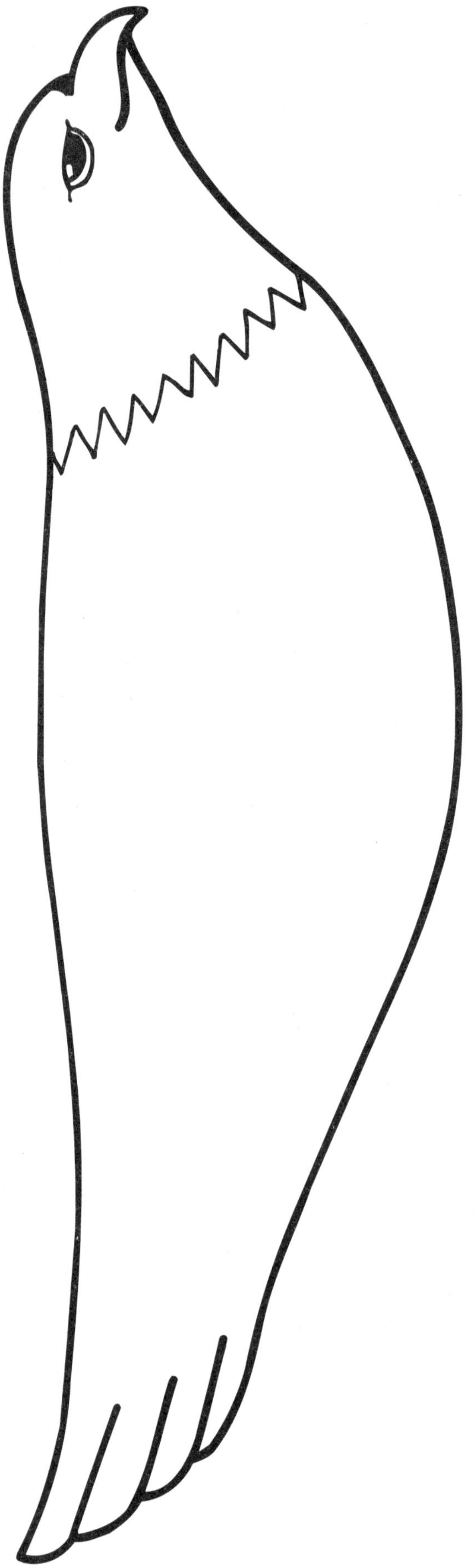

A TRIBUTE TO TRIBES

American Indian Day was first celebrated in New York on May 13, 1916. The purpose of this special occasion was to recognize and honor American Indians and to help improve their condition. Sherman Coolidge, an Arapahoe Indian and president of the American Indian Association at the time, asked that the day be observed "as one set apart as a memorial to the red race of America and to a wise consideration of its future." Today, the second Saturday in May is set aside to pay tribute to Native Americans in 10 states throughout the nation.

A second holiday honoring American Indians is held on September 23, and is called Native American Day. This special day was designated in 1912 by Arthur C. Parker to honor the people who first settled the continent. Parker was a descendant of Seneca Indians.

BodyArt activities in this unit are designed to help young children appreciate the Native American culture: its spirit, customs, attitude toward nature, belief in the extended family, and emphasis on family ties. At unit's end, each child will have had the experience of being a papoose, wearing moccasins, creating a sand painting, making a rain stick, and learning about tribal homes. Have fun as you share this very special tribute to tribes with the children!

Happy Little Papooses Bulletin Board

This special bulletin board is the perfect place for your papooses to start learning about Native Americans—nestled in their cozy traveling beds!

Materials: Close-up photos of the children, scissors, pencil, brown and orange construction paper, glue, white poster board, markers or crayons, transparent tape

Directions: Ask children to bring in close-up photos of themselves or snap pictures of them yourself. Set aside. Trace each child's foot on a sheet of brown or orange construction paper and cut out. Round off the toe area. Now cut out the face portion of each photo to fit in the heel area of the paper feet. Glue each photo to the child's paper foot. Let the children decorate their traveling beds with markers or crayons. Then tape the completed beds to the poster board. Each child may take his or her papoose bed home at the end of the unit.

↑ glue photo to foot and decorate

Walk-a-Mile Moccasins

They say you don't really know someone until you've walked a mile in his or her shoes. These *BodyArt* shoes are moccasins, and the children can decide whether to make them plain or fancy.

Materials: Brown and white construction paper, masking tape, scissors, markers, crayons, pencil, child's shoes

Directions: Trace the child's feet on brown or white construction paper. Cut out the paper feet and smooth out the toe area. Let the child decorate the tracings with markers or crayons. Moccasins often feature turquoise and red beadwork, yellow sections, and geometric designs, but the child can decide on the shapes and colors to use.

When the moccasins are ready, press a piece of rolled masking tape to the back of each paper foot. Press the paper feet onto the top of the child's shoes. Encourage the child to walk around in the moccasins and pretend to be a member of a Native American tribe.

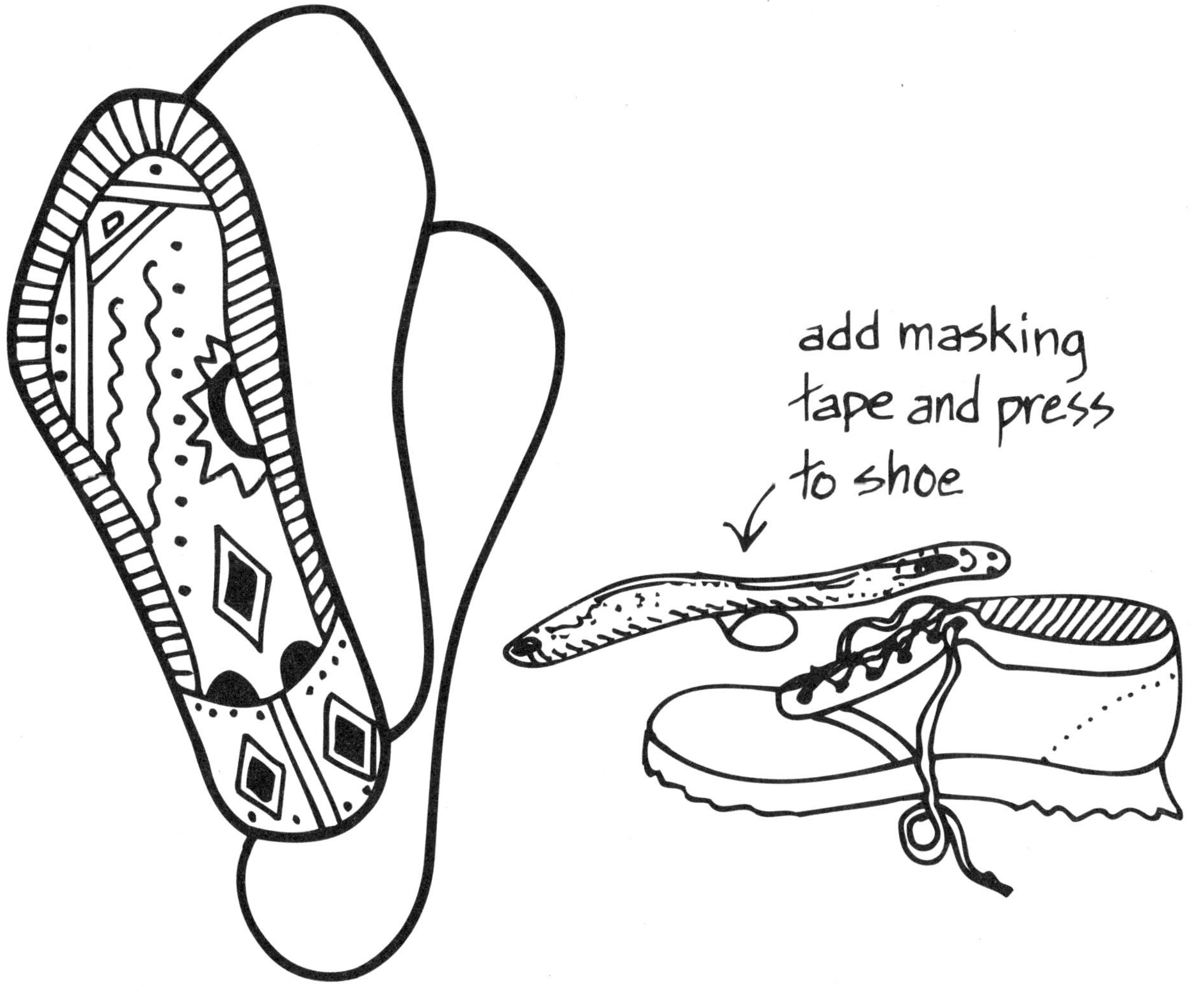

add masking tape and press to shoe

Sand Hand Hanging

Certain tribes believe creating sand paintings is part of a very private ritual that shouldn't be shared. Others don't mind showing others this fascinating process. The *BodyArt* sand painting is the perfect combination of the process and the creator—a sand painting of the artist's hand!

Materials: Colored sand, large paper plate, pencil, hole punch, yarn or ribbon, brush, nontoxic glue, stickers (optional)

Directions: Trace the child's hand in the center of a large paper plate. Trace over the outline with glue. Pour colored sand carefully over the outline, then dust off and save any sand that doesn't stick to the glue. Set aside for a minute or two to dry.

Next, brush glue over the palm area of the paper hand. Pour colored sand over that area and dust off, again saving any extra sand. After the glue has completely dried, punch a hole in the top center of the paper plate. Loop an 8" piece of yard or ribbon through the hole. Double the yarn and tie in a bow. If desired, add teddy bear, star, heart, and other self-adhesive stickers around the perimeter of the plate. The sand painting can be displayed on the classroom wall or hung in the child's window at home.

Rain Stick

Native American tribes, especially those that farm the land, have always been concerned about rainfall. When rain doesn't fall for a period of time, a ceremony that incorporates the use of a rain stick is held to encourage it.

Materials: Empty paper towel tube; scissors; nontoxic glue; nontoxic, washable tempera paint (earth colors); 8 1/2" by 11" sheet of white or light-colored construction paper; masking tape; transparent tape; sand; dry beans; shallow paint trays; brush; measuring cup

Directions: Ask the child to dip his or her palm into a tray of paint. Then have the child make hand prints on white or light-colored construction paper. Finger imprints may be added for further decoration. Set aside the paper to dry. Now tape one end of the paper towel tube completely closed with masking tape. Fill the tube with a half-cup of sand and six or seven dry beans. Seal the other end of the tube with masking tape.

To cover the tube with the decorated construction paper, brush nontoxic glue over the tube's entire surface. Carefully press and roll on the hand imprint sheet. Trim as needed. When the rain stick is dry, have the rain dancer shake it and watch the raindrops fall!

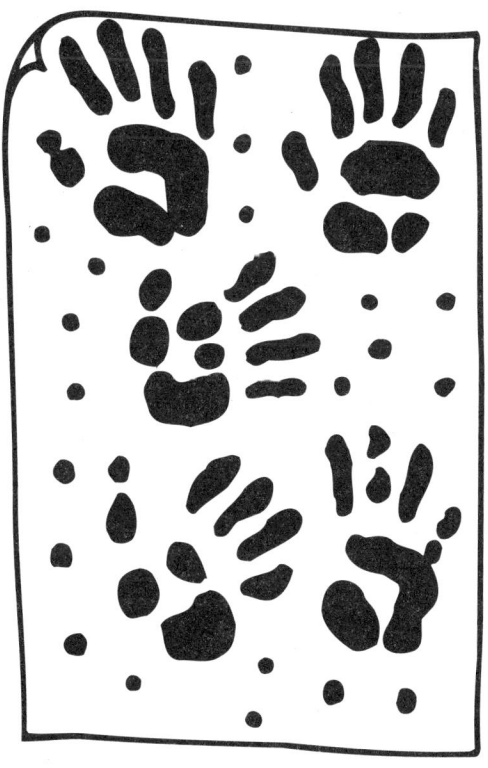

cover with glue-press and roll on paper

A Tribute to Tribes Finger Plays and Movement Songs

Tribe Counting Song
(to the tune of "Ten Little Indians")

One peaceful, two peaceful, three peaceful Navajos,
Four dancing, five dancing, six dancing Seminoles,
Seven wise, eight wise, nine wise Iroquois,
Ten tribal members all!

Indian Homes

(Before reciting this action verse, copy and color the Indian home reproducibles on pp. 65-68. Then let the children hold up the appropriate home when it is mentioned. By teaching children that Native Americans don't all live in tepees, one stereotype is addressed and, hopefully, corrected.)

I'm a Woodland Indian and I live in a wigwam.
(Hold up wigwam.)
Tall trees and bark keep me warm in winter.
(Reach for sky, then smile and look cozy.)
I am a member of the Sac-Fox tribe.

I'm a Southwest Indian and I live in a pueblo.
(Hold up pueblo.)
Adobe brick keeps me cool in summer.
(Fan face, then make circle for the sun.)
I am a member of the Hopi tribe.

I'm a Western Prairie Indian and I live in an earth lodge.
(Hold up earth lodge.)
Grass and tree trunks keep me dry in rainstorms.
(Move hands up and down for rain, then shelter head with hands.)
I am a member of the Pawnee tribe.

I'm a Plains Indian and I live in a tepee.
(Hold up tepee.)
Hides and poles keep me safe at night.
(Make "going to bed" motions with hands.)
I am a member of the Blackfoot tribe.

Mother Earth, Father Sky Song

(to the tune of "Billy Boy")

Oh, where have you been, Mother Earth, Mother Earth?
Where have you been, Mother Earth?
I've been dancing with tribes,
They're the joy of my life.
Tribes know how to take care of fields and flowers.

Oh, where have you been, Father Sky, Father Sky?
Where have you been, Father Sky?
I've been flying with tribes,
They're the joy of my life.
Tribes know how to take care of hawks and eagles.

Oh, where have you been, Sister Stream, Sister Stream?
Where have you been, Sister Stream?
I've been swimming with tribes,
They're the joy of my life.
Tribes know how to take care of water creatures.

Oh, where have you been, Brother Fire, Brother Fire?
Where have you been, Brother Fire?
I've been dining with tribes,
They're the joy of my life.
Tribes know how to take care of one another.

A Tribute to Tribes Read-Alouds

Fiction

Baker, Olaf. *Where the Buffaloes Begin.* New York: Puffin Books, 1981.

A Caldecott Honor book, this realistic fiction offering has beautiful black and white illustrations by Stephen Gammell. Little Wolf goes to the lake where the buffaloes begin and becomes a hero in his own right.

Baylor, Byrd. *Hawk, I'm Your Brother.* New York: Aladdin Books, 1976.

This Caldecott Honor book, illustrated by Peter Parnall, tells about the relationship between Rudy Soto and a hawk. Rudy wants to soar through the air like the powerful bird, and thinks he can learn the secrets of flying by capturing it.

Baylor, Byrd. *The Way to Start a Day.* New York: Macmillan, 1978.

This Caldecott Honor book shows how Native Americans appreciate Earth's morning majesty.

Cohen, Caron Lee. *The Mud Pony.* New York: Scholastic, 1988.

This traditional Skidi Pawnee tale tells about a poor boy who longs to own a pony of his own. When he fashions one out of mud, he begins a lifelong relationship with Mother Earth.

de Paola, Tomie. *The Legend of the Bluebonnet.* New York: Putnam's, 1983.

A drought threatens to destroy a tribe until a small girl named She-Who-Is-Alone sacrifices her favorite possession to save her people.

Goble, Paul. *Iktomi and the Boulder.* New York: Trumpet Club, 1988.

A Plains Indian tale that tells one of many stories about the hero Iktomi (eek-toe-me). Young children can learn the names of Native American items, including feather bonnets, fans, and blankets, in addition to listening to a new story.

Hayes, Joe. *Coyote and the Butterflies.* New York: Scholastic, 1993.

Available as a Big Book in the Multicultural Tale series, the story relays how a lazy coyote sleeps while his wife works hard all day. He doesn't get away with it, however, because butterflies play a trick on him.

Jeffers, Susan (illustrator). *Brother Eagle, Sister Sky.* New York: Dial, 1991.

The story of Chief Seattle's reply to the new Commissioner of Indian Affairs long ago is as beautiful as poetry; it begins, "How can you buy the sky?" Susan Jeffers' paintings are a wonderful complement.

Longfellow, Henry Wadsworth. *Hiawatha.* New York: Scholastic, 1983.

Susan Jeffers' illustrations add a new dimension and sensitivity to the Longfellow epic poem.

Martin, Jr., Bill and John Archambault. *Knots on a Counting Rope.* New York: Holt, 1987.

A visually challenged boy loves to hear his grandfather talk about how he was given his name, "Boy-Strength-of-Blue-Horses."

McDermott, Gerald. *Arrow to the Sun.* New York: Viking, 1977.

Young children will especially love the story and pictures that are part of this Pueblo Indian tale. The Caldecott Medal winner tells about a boy's search for his father.

Osofsky, Audrey. *Dreamcatcher.* New York: Orchard Books, 1992.

Beautiful, haunting illustrations by Ed Young enhance the author's story about how bad dreams are caught.

Nonfiction

Baylor, Byrd. *When Clay Sings.* New York: Scribner's, 1972.

A Caldecott Honor offering about how pieces of prehistoric Indian pottery help reconstruct a tribe's daily way of life.

Caduto, Michael J. and Joseph Bruchac. *Keepers of the Earth.* Golden, Colo.: Fulcrum, 1989.

Native American legends and environmental activities for children are included in this rich resource book.

de Paola, Tomie. *The Popcorn Book.* New York: Holiday House, 1978.

Master storyteller and illustrator de Paola tells enough about popcorn to answer young children's questions.

Goble, Paul. *The Gift of the Sacred Dog.* Scarsdale, New York: Bradbury Press, 1980.

This wonderfully illustrated book describes how horses were brought to North America by the Spanish.

Lopez, Alonzo. *Celebration.* Littleton, Mass.: Sundance Publishers & Distributors, 1972.

Illustrations from a variety of artists help tell the story of how tribal dancing, fire making, and game playing are part of a tribe's celebration.

Peters, Russell. *Regalia.* Littleton, Mass.: Sundance Publishers & Distributors, 1992.

Native American costumes and dances are brought to children through these excellent pictures. Stereotypes are broken down by the introduction of readers to the "real" people beneath the ritual masks and elaborate costumes.

A Tribute to Tribes Snacktime

Have a Popcorn Party!

Some say corn is the Native American gift to the world. Thousands of years ago it was called maize, and it didn't look a lot like our present-day golden variety. Now there are lots of different varieties of popcorn—a healthy snack if you don't drench it in salt and melted butter or margarine. Try out some recipes from Tomie de Paola's *The Popcorn Book*. Whichever one you choose, it's bound to be a "pop-ular" snack with children!

A Tribute to Tribes Game

Popping Up and Down

Watching popcorn kernels pop in a hot-air popcorn machine is a good way to show children how to "pop" up and down during this game. In addition to having a good-old "corny" time, the game helps to improve directional skills.

Tell the children that the popcorn machine is ready to heat up the popcorn. Have the children start popping up and down. Then have an adult tell them to pop left and pop right. Children should continue to jump up and down, but also move to a designated space in the appropriate direction. Vary the directions, including back/forth, here/there; you can also introduce fast/slow, happy/sad, and the full range of movements and emotions. After two or three minutes, turn the popcorn machine off. The children should pop slower and slower and then come to a stop.

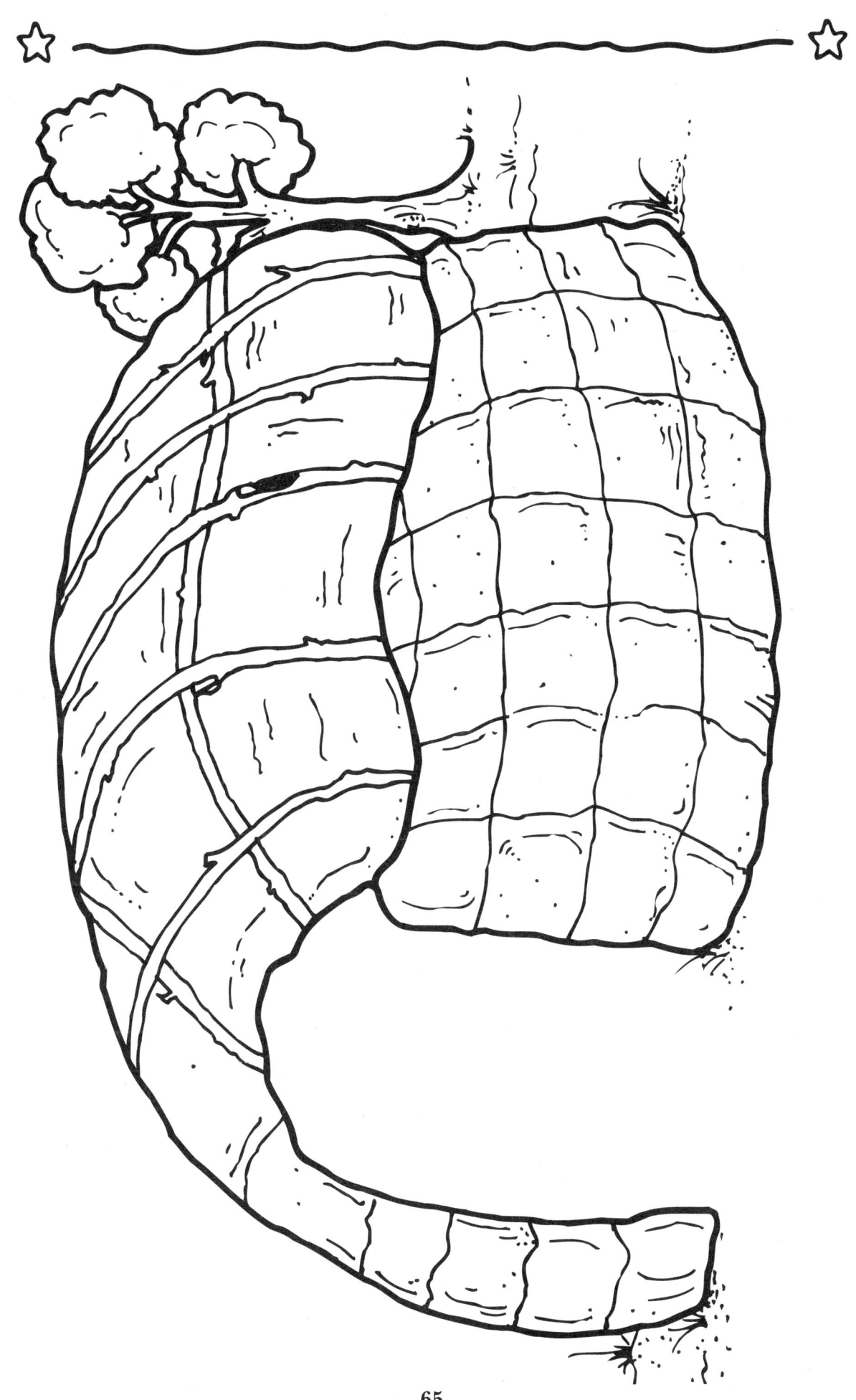

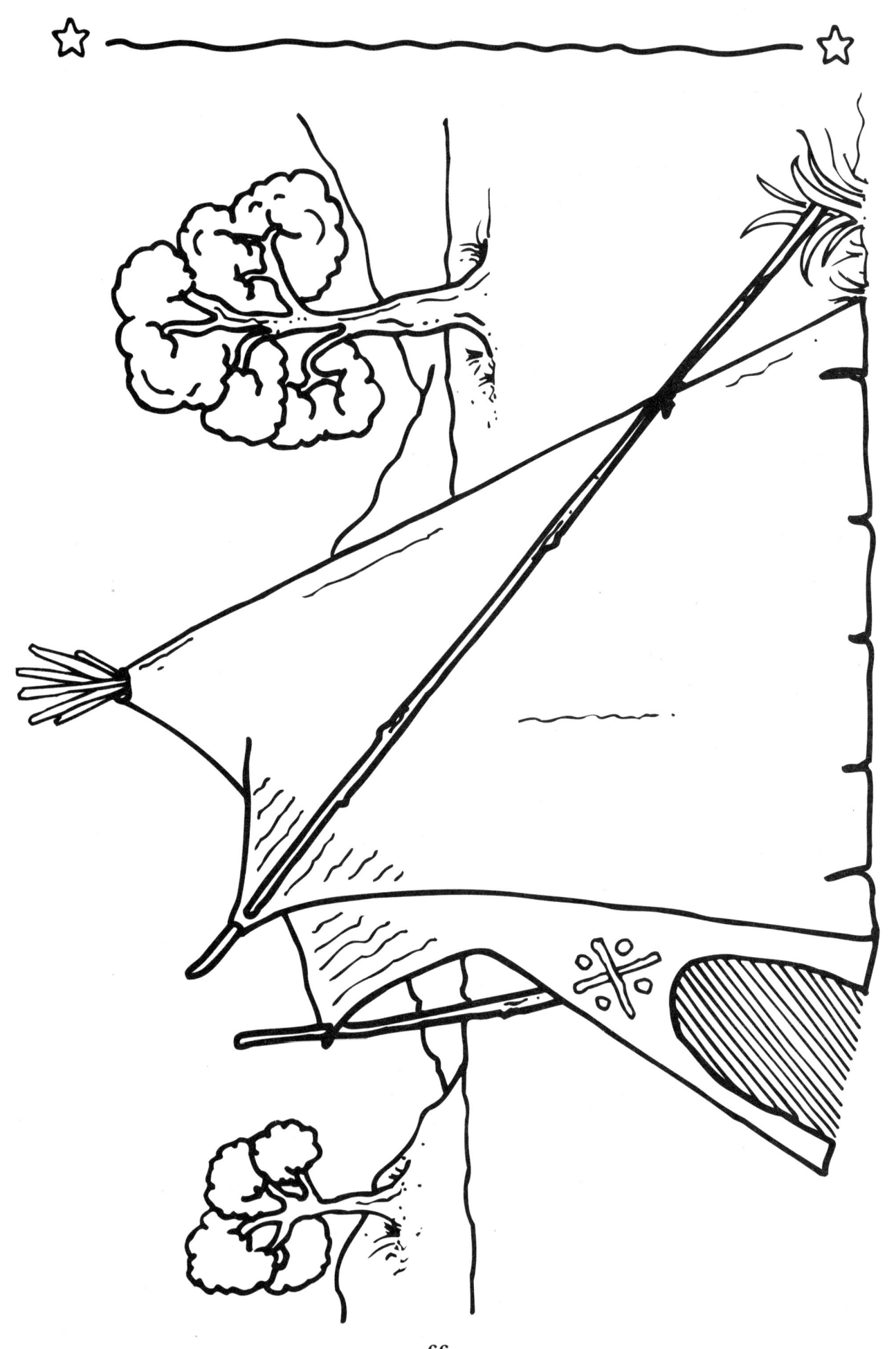

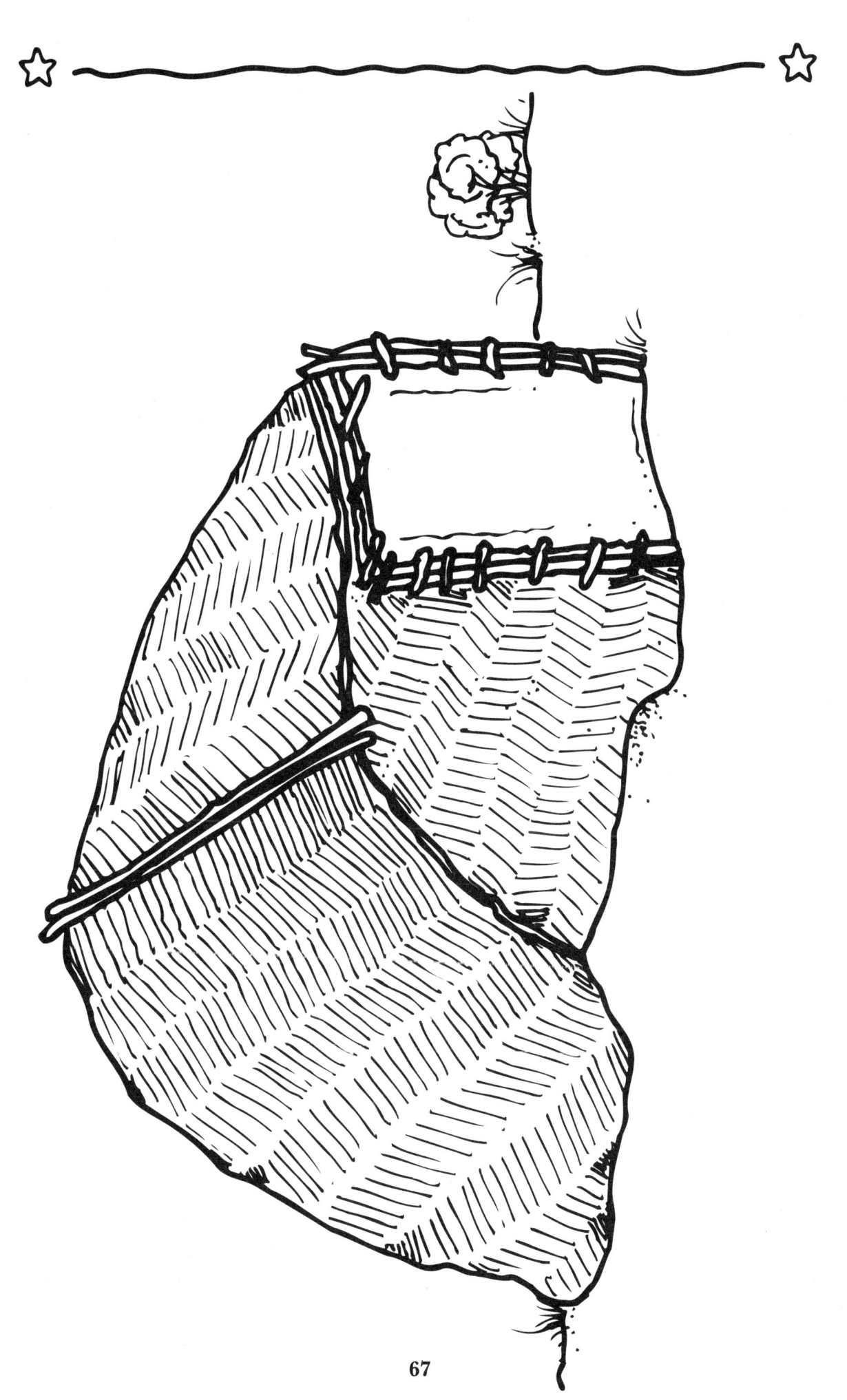

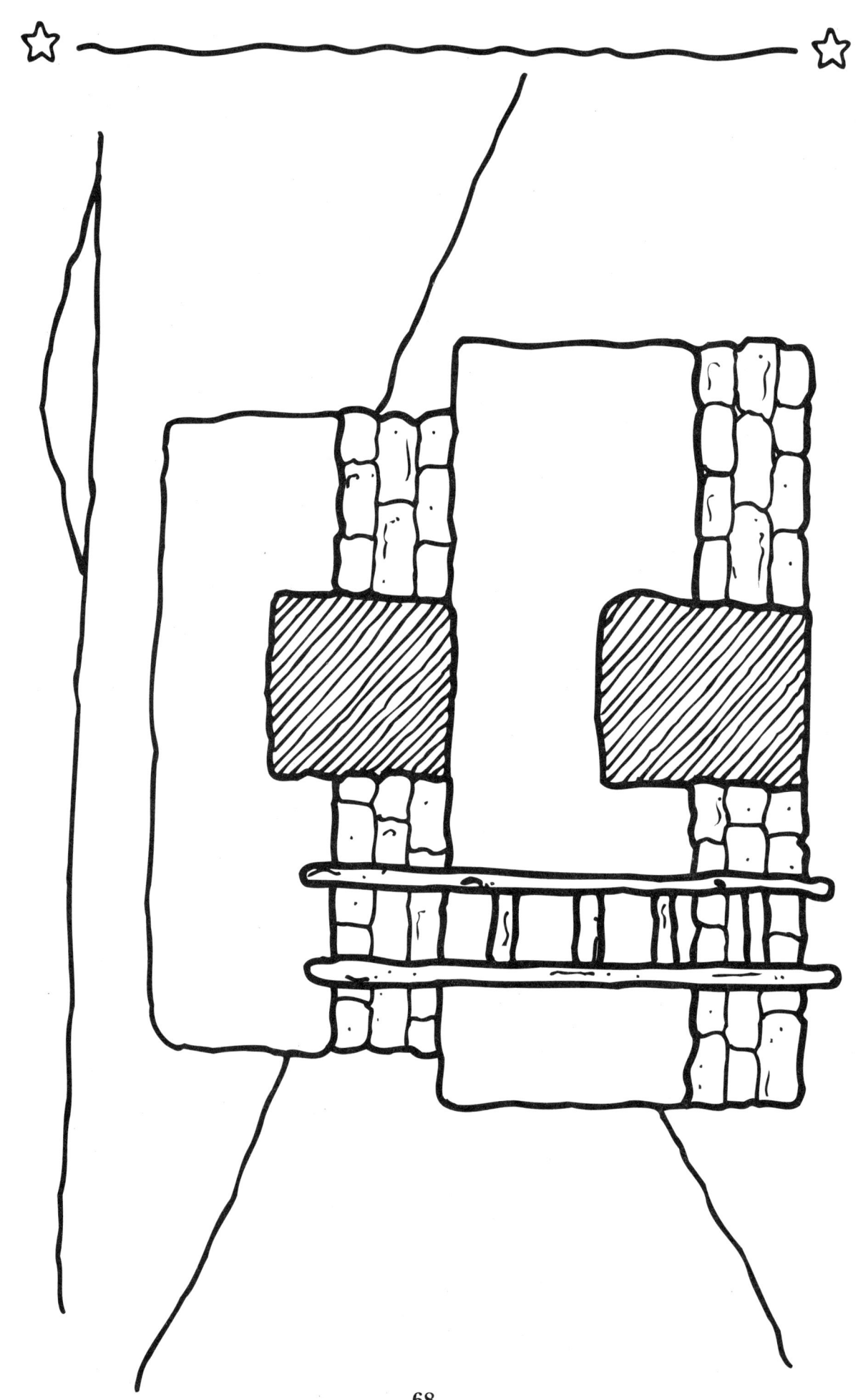

HAPPY BIRTHDAY, AMERICA!

Every summer Americans celebrate the birth of their nation on the Fourth of July—Independence Day. Back in 1776, the Continental Congress adopted the Declaration of Independence and declared the colonies to be free and independent states—the United States of America.

This *BodyArt* chapter has star-spangled activities that young children will enjoy. Naturally, the red, white, and blue of the American flag figure prominently in them, as do the elements of freedom and independence, represented in the *BodyArt* Liberty Bell and Lady Liberty Crown. And since summer is traditionally a festive, warm season, children will also make a Patriotic Ice Cream Cone in this fun-filled unit.

Let Freedom Ring Bulletin Board

In colonial America, the bell was a very important means of communicating news throughout neighboring towns and villages. In Philadelphia, one famous bell, the Liberty Bell, rang out America's newly declared independence. The bell is now a reminder to us to believe in and cherish our freedom just as America's forefathers did more than 200 years ago.

Materials: Red and blue construction paper, scissors, pencil, white poster board, hole punch, paper fastener

Directions: Trace the child's hand (fingers together) on a sheet of red or blue construction paper. Cut out the paper hand. Repeat six or seven times, varying the construction paper colors so that the completed board has a red, white, and blue look to it. Punch a hole in the upper palm area of each paper hand "bell." Insert a paper fastener and secure behind the poster board. The bells should be able to move back and forth, just like real bells!

Option: Add real bells to the paper ones so that they can ring when they're moved. You may also want to glue small American flags, found in craft and party stores, to the board.

Ring Out Liberty Bell

Here's a variation of the bulletin board bell that is suitable for children to take home.

Materials: Medium-sized bell (available at craft stores); red, white, and blue construction paper; clear self-adhesive plastic; scissors; hole punch; pencil; yarn; small self-adhesive American flags (optional)

Directions: Trace the child's hand (fingers together) on a sheet of construction paper. Cut out the paper hand and decorate the center with an American flag if desired. Cover the paper "bell" with clear self-adhesive plastic for durability. Then punch a hole in the finger area. Loop a 6" piece of strong yarn through the hole and double it. Tie a bell onto the yarn and knot securely. Punch a second hole at the base of the palm area and tie a yarn bow through it. To ring the bell, turn it so the bow is at the top and gently move it back and forth. *Note:* Be sure young children aren't able to reach loose bells and put them in their mouths.

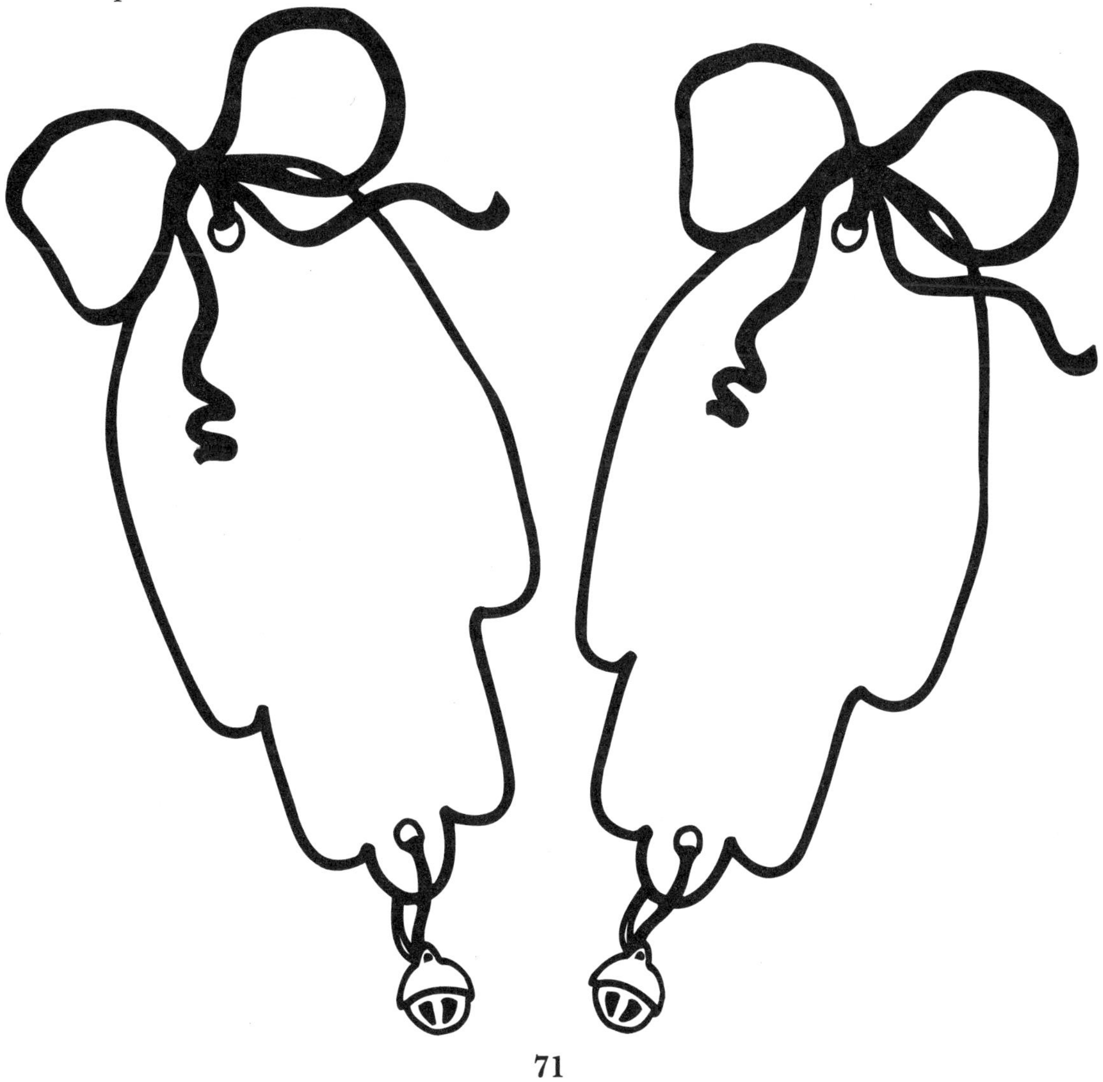

Lady Liberty Crown

The Statue of Liberty, or Lady Liberty, as she is often called, was a gift to America from France in 1886. Sculptor Frédéric Auguste Bartholdi constructed the classical goddess dressed in the clothes of ancient Greece (the birthplace of democracy), and gave her a torch (the light of liberty) to carry and a crown (with seven spokes representing the seven continents and seas) to wear.

Materials: Large paper plate; scissors; pencil; green and white non-toxic, washable tempera; staples and stapler; tagboard or poster board; brush; paint trays

Directions: Cut a circle out of the center of a large paper plate. Make the hole large enough to fit on a child's head. Make spokes by tracing the child's hand (fingers apart) on a sheet of tagboard or poster board four times. Cut out the paper hands. To paint the crown and spokes, use authentic-looking copper-green paint made by mixing one part green to one part white paint. Let dry completely. Staple the base of the paper hands to the crown rim, gently bending the hands so that the paper fingers extend upward. Let the child wear the crown while playing the "Liberty Statues" game (p. 78).

Patriotic Ice Cream Cone

What would a hot Fourth of July day be without a frozen (then melting!) confection!

Materials: Ice cream cone reproducible (p. 79); white poster board; nontoxic glue; scissors; cardboard; glue; brown, red, and blue crayons or markers; red sticky dots (optional)

Directions: Copy, color, and cut out the ice cream cone reproducible. To make it more durable, glue a piece of cardboard to the back. Then trace the child's hand (fingers apart) on a sheet of white poster board. Use markers (and red sticky dots, if desired) to add "blueberry topping" and a round red "cherry" to the top of the paper hand "ice cream." Cut out and glue this confection to the cone reproducible with the paper fingers extending downward, as though the ice cream was melting. Even if it is, this patriotic cone will last a long, long time!

use markers to add cherry and topping

Happy Birthday, America!
Finger Plays and Movement Songs

The Fourth of July Song
(to the tune of "Row, Row, Row Your Boat")

Happy, happy, happy birthday,
It's America's day.
Every year on the Fourth of July
We celebrate all day!

There are lots of marching bands
And fireworks at night.
Bright colors fill the sky—
It's such a pretty sight!

I'm a Little Candle
(to the tune of "I'm a Little Teapot")

I'm a little candle, tall and proud.
Where I am sitting
Children shout out loud!

They are so happy I am here
To celebrate
With birthday cheer!

Whose birthday is it, can you guess?
Our country's birthday—
Yes, yes, yes!

Marching in the Big Parade
(to the tune of "The Bear Went Over the Mountain")

We're marching in the parade,
We're marching in the parade,
We're marching in the parade
For America's birthday!

We're skipping in the parade,
We're skipping in the parade,
We're skipping in the parade
For America's birthday!

We're tiptoeing in the parade,
We're tiptoeing in the parade,
We're tiptoeing in the parade
For America's birthday!

We're jumping in the parade,
We're jumping in the parade,
We're jumping in the parade
For America's birthday!

We're hopping in the parade,
We're hopping in the parade,
We're hopping in the parade
For America's birthday!

Happy Birthday, America Song

(to the tune of "Here We Go 'Round the Mulberry Bush")

Happy birthday, America,
America, America.
Happy birthday, America,
It's a special day.

It's a day for us to cheer,
Us to cheer, us to cheer.
It's a day for us to cheer
And sing and dance and play.

It's a day to wave the flag,
Wave the flag, wave the flag.
It's a day to wave the flag
And sing and dance and play.

(To accompany this song, reproduce the flag on p. 80. Tape each flag to a dowel or Popsicle stick.)

Happy Birthday, America! Read-Alouds

Fiction

Anno, Mitsumasa. *Anno's U.S.A.* New York: Philomel Books, 1983.

This wordless picture book with wonderful illustrations shows a traveler going east across the U.S.

Brown, M. K. *Let's Go Swimming with Mr. Sillypants.* New York: Crown, 1986.

Okay, it's not about America, but the book ties in with the summer festivities that abound during this special holiday. This well-loved silly story is about Mr. Sillypants, who lives by the ocean but has never learned to swim.

Bunting, Eve. *How Many Days to America?* New York: Trumpet Club, 1988.

A serious but lovely story about immigrants who flee for their lives and come to America.

Sandin, Joan. *The Long Way to a New Land.* New York: Harper & Row, 1981.

This story tells about how a man named Carl Erik came to America in 1868 to escape the famine in Sweden.

Nonfiction

Spier, Peter. *The Star-Spangled Banner.* New York: Trumpet Club, 1973.

This "Reading Rainbow"-featured book makes the song come alive with wonderful pictures.

Happy Birthday, America! Snacktime

Red, White, and Blue Cake

Why not celebrate America's birthday with your favorite white cake? Just follow your favorite white cake recipe, then add red food coloring to white frosting and spread it on. Top with blue candles and sing "Happy Birthday" before you blow them out!

Parfait Sparkler

Serve up this cool treat on a hot day. In a plastic cup for each child, place a scoop of vanilla ice cream or frozen yogurt. Add a thin layer of crunchy granola, then follow with a sprinkling of flavorful blueberries or blackberries. Complete the red, white, and blue creation with a bright red maraschino cherry or pitted fresh cherry. Hand out plastic spoons and direct the group to a shady outdoor snacking spot.

add crunchy granola, then blueberries

Happy Birthday, America! Game

Liberty Statues

Here's a good way to incorporate the *BodyArt* Statue of Liberty Crowns in a very exciting game!

Directions: Ask children to put on their Lady Liberty Crowns (p. 72). Then tell them that they can move around to the music you play until the music stops. At that point they become Statues of Liberty and must "freeze" in place. Those who move after the music stops are not removed from the game, but simply take off their crowns and keep on playing. This more child-friendly version encourages cooperation rather than competition, prevents feelings from being hurt, and bolsters self-esteem.